Youth Work Ethics

Youth Work Ethics

Howard Sercombe

Los Angeles | London | New Delhi
Singapore | Washington DC

SAGE Publications Ltd
1 Oliver's Yard
55 City Road
London EC1Y 1SP

SAGE Publications Inc.
2455 Teller Road
Thousand Oaks, California 91320

SAGE Publications India Pvt Ltd
B 1/I 1 Mohan Cooperative Industrial Area
Mathura Road
New Delhi 110 044

SAGE Publications Asia-Pacific Pte Ltd
33 Pekin Street #02-01
Far East Square
Singapore 048763

Library of Congress Control Number: 2009931922

British Library Cataloguing in Publication data

A catalogue record for this book is available from the British Library

ISBN 978-1-84787-603-4
ISBN 978-1-84787-604-1 (pbk)

Typeset by C&M Digitals (P) Ltd, Chennai, India
Printed and bound Great Britain by TJ International Ltd, Padstow, Cornwall
Printed on paper from sustainable resources

This book is dedicated to Helen Wolfenden. Her support and encouragement has been unstinting, and there have been many times where she has carried the load of life outside the book while I buried myself in it. Her passion for truth and her unerring nose for inauthenticity and self-deception, so important in my own journey, might also mean that this book contains fewer hypocrisies than it otherwise would.

CONTENTS

Part One

The Youth Work Profession

1

INTRODUCTION

The intention of this book is to engage in a conversation about the core ethics of youth work as a profession. It isn't the first conversation about this: for youth workers, the ethical dimension is never far from the surface (Young 2006, Sapin 2009). All the things that youth work claims to do and to be for young people are about the ethics of the situation. Social justice is an ethical requirement. Empowerment is an ethical project. Inclusion is ethically driven. Poverty, homelessness, violence, destructive drug use, dispossession… these aren't technical problems, awaiting the skill and resource to fix them. They are deeply moral issues. To use that most unfashionable of words, their continued existence, and the structures that maintain them, are *wrong*. The reason that many of us got into youth work, and the reason we stayed, is because of that.

But these conversations haven't always happened overtly within an ethics framework. Over the last few years there have been stronger attempts to be more consistent in our thinking, and to connect our thinking to wider conversations about ethics as a philosophical discipline, especially in the field of professional ethics (see Banks 1999, Roberts 2009). And to work harder to develop shared, articulate positions on common ethical questions.

There is a wide range of perspectives on the relationship between a practice and its ethics. Much of this work, building on Ernest Greenwood's classic essay (1957), identified the professions by a list of attributes, with ethics one attribute among many (such as formal training, a licence to practise, processes for registration and deregistration). However, in a pivotal piece of scholarship published in 1994, Daryl Koehn argued that ethics is not one of several *attributes* of the professions. Ethics is the core, it is what makes a profession a profession.

This position changes our understanding of ethics and the professions. From this perspective, ethics is not primarily about *prohibition*, about lists of things one should not do. It is about *identity*, what we claim, what constitutes us. The essence of youth work is its ethics.

While this book is grounded in youth work practice, it also takes theory seriously. The theory has mostly come from the discipline of moral philosophy. The issues that moral philosophers are interested in are often frustratingly distant from the day-to-day practice of youth workers, but the theoretical thinking is, and continues to be, useful. That is where I have gone to find the kind of disciplined language that will work for youth work, that will sharpen and strengthen our thinking, and that will call us out when we are kidding ourselves.

Sometimes, we won't be comfortable with that language. I try to translate and adapt where I can, but some terms don't translate. The term 'client' is an example of that (see Chapter 3). Youth workers (particularly in the UK) are typically put off by connotations of inferiority or condescension that they feel in the word, and there are good reasons for that, particularly in the history of the helping professions. We'll try to work with that and other similar problems as the argument progresses. However, readers will find in this book a struggle for precision in what words like that *mean*, rather than whether they are popular or not.

The book also tries to be international, engaging with the ethics of practice at least across the UK (and England, Wales, Scotland and Northern Ireland all have their differences), Australia and New Zealand as well as North America. Each of these has its own way of thinking about youth work, and its own languages for talking about practice, and there are distinct sensitivities in each. In each context, youth workers are responding to and being shaped by different funding and policy agendas, which themselves change continuously. Some I understand better than others. But while the way that youth workers talk about their practice can be very different across the planet and across time, the way their practice feels, the way it 'smells' if you like, is congruent.

I try to engage with that core, though readers may find that the language is not immediately familiar or conventional or aligned with current policy where they are. Where I can, I try to avoid jargon, to speak directly and simply, or to use concepts that belong to no particular setting at the moment but might be useful across settings. Youth work has been around for 150 years (Davies 1999): a book like this needs to still be relevant when governments, policy settings and priorities have changed, as they do so often.

The book is set out in three sections. Part One explores the idea of a profession, and the place of youth work among the professions. The conversation is important because it establishes not only what we *do* but what we *are*. Zygmunt Bauman (1992) argues that truth in the (post) modern world is established by our own commitment to it. The ethical claims of youth work then become real and true because collectively we affirm, assert and commit ourselves to those ethical objectives.

Part Two mines the body of philosophical writing about ethics, covering method and theory in thinking about ethics. The major schools of thinking are canvassed (though all too briefly and with many variations left out) along with their strengths and weaknesses. Each of them has attempted at various points in history to assert itself as the one truth about ethics. I have my own preferences, as you will discover, but theory is a conceptual toolbox to break open situations, work them out, and work out what is to be done, not a set of divine and unalterable pronouncements. Different situations call for different tools, and, as much as we can, I want to keep the dialogue open between these very different approaches to working out what is important and what ought to be done. The role and utility of Codes of Ethics in shaping professional practice is part of that conversation.

Part Three deals with a range of common ethical issues and conflicts in our practice. Broadly, these mirror the issues that most codes of ethics are concerned to deal with, though hopefully these chapters will be much more than a commentary on the standard set of clauses in professional codes of ethics. Because focused writing on ethics from within youth work is so scant, we'll raid the other professions for what insights they have, as well as reflecting on experience within my own practice and that of my colleagues over the years. In the process of working through the dilemmas that youth workers face every day, this section attempts also to define and describe what an authentic youth work response might look like: again, addressing not only our behaviour, but our identity. Sometimes, this section will read like a youth work manual. To some extent that is unavoidable, if youth work is constituted by its ethics. But it is not the intention of this book to lay down youth work *method*, even though we will talk all the time about practice. Readers who are looking for guidance about youth work method will find lots of gaps.

It is clear that this is not a book that tries to be dispassionately objective. You might have worked that out already. I am a youth worker. I have been a youth worker all my working life, and all my professional thinking, theory development and research has happened within that commitment. Many of the perspectives and insights in this book come out of that history, out of my own experience and of those I have worked with and shared with, across three continents. That history has not always necessarily been pretty. Plenty of whatever wisdom might have ended up in this book has come out of seeing too late that I have crossed a line (or knowing exactly where the line was and convincing myself that it was excusable cross it) and often enough, the damage which has followed.

As a youth worker, I am partisan. While this book is written for youth workers, it is not primarily the interests of youth workers that are at its heart. It is the interests of young people, particularly the most dispossessed, which define our practice. Young people deserve the best, most creative, most disciplined, most informed, most thoughtful, most compassionate connection that we can provide. This book is a conversation with youth workers that hopes to contribute to that end. As such, it is not *about* youth work ethics. It is, or tries to be, a youth work ethics. It is certainly not the only possible youth work ethics, but a sustained, applied ethical argument nonetheless.

The attempt by one person to write that ethics is presumptive, I know. It is unlikely that I have got it right for practitioners across several continents and a bewildering range of practice contexts and ideological positions, particularly when I have spent so little time especially with colleagues outside Australia, New Zealand and the UK. We youth workers tend to resist definition and 'being boxed' almost as a point of principle. However, across our different national contexts, the call for clarity in articulation of our practice is universal. Hopefully, this narrative – of a profession constituted by its commitment to young people as its primary client, working with them in their social context to facilitate their ethical agency, and with their society to clear barriers of oppression and exclusion – is useful, and will work for some, giving them a clarity of purpose and solidarity with others likewise committed.

Some acknowledgments. My own development has been shaped by some fine youth work minds: Greg and Rosemary Miller, John West, George Davies,

Chris Brown, Jim Punton, Morris Stuart, Suzi Quixley, Jeremy Prince, Peter Logan, Jethro Sercombe, and supervisors like Graham Chipps and Neil Hamilton. And lots of Ethics in Youth Work students. It has taken the encouragement of Doug Magnusson and Helen Wolfenden to get me to write. Valuable critical comment has come from Jon Ord, Sarah Banks, Helen Wolfenden, Susannah Trefgarne, Emma Patterson, and a number of anonymous reviewers. Time for the book, and testing ideas within it, has been supported by my colleagues at the University of Strathclyde. Any mistakes or omissions in this book, and the existence of the book itself, are therefore entirely their fault and I take no responsibility for them whatsoever.

2

ETHICS AND THE IDEA OF A PROFESSION

Summary

The question of an ethics for youth work implies the question of youth work as a profession, just by virtue of the long association between thinking about professions and thinking about ethics. This chapter explores the idea of a 'profession' – both what professions are in practice, and what they should be in principle – from an ethical point of view. The conclusion is that in these terms, youth work is a profession, whether or not it is recognised as one and whether or not it organises itself that way.

As the first chapter indicates, this book is primarily interested in youth work ethics, not youth work as a profession. Like many youth workers, I have always been ambivalent on the question of whether youth work ought to consider itself a profession and whether it ought to organise itself as one (Walker 2002; Banks 2004). But you can't go far in an exploration of one without being confronted with the other. What you do with that depends greatly on how you define what a profession is and how you analyse the way a profession works.

A lot of the primary work on the professions has been done by sociologists, rather than philosophers (e.g. Durkheim 1957). As sociologists, their primary concern was to look at the professions in terms of their social function, their role in the economy, and the ways that professional status was able to leverage power. Their approach was to study the existing professions, identifying the features they had in common, and the way they worked on the ground.

The work was difficult, given the number of professions and the number of occupations aspiring to be professions, and the manifold complexity of the way that professions work in practice. Many of their judgements were harsh. According to commentators like Illich and his collaborators (1977), the professions operate as self-interested associations of the privileged (or aspiring thereto) who organise in order to:

- restrict entry to the profession, and therefore artificially inflate their own incomes by maintaining scarcity of professional labour,
- use their collective power to promote their own interests,
- make professionals less, not more, accountable by mystifying processes that are in themselves easy to understand,

- disempower clients through the use of jargon and technical language, which puts their business out of their own reach, and
- protect each other by closing ranks when complaints are made against their members.

This analysis points out how corrupt the professions are, how they masquerade as something noble while acting as a vehicle for the greed of their members, and how they all support the *status quo*. Or, as George Bernard Shaw once said, 'every profession is a conspiracy against the laity' (Koehn 1994: 1). (We'll look at the question of corruption in Chapter 17.)

The key positive legacy of the research was a way of defining the professions by listing their common traits. Greenwood's (1957) influential paper, for example, used a kind of 'ideal type' analysis to paint a picture of the 'typical' or 'iconic' profession, based on the features that most professions had, or at least those that everyone agreed were professions. Occupations were deemed to be professions to the degree that they possessed these common traits. Others were classified as para-professions or quasi-professions or emerging professions.

Greenwood's key attributes of a profession

A profession is a social grouping with:

- a systematic body of knowledge
- professional authority and credibility
- regulation and control of its members
- a professional code of ethics
- a culture of values, norms and symbols.

(Greenwood 1957)

A different idea of what a profession is

The problem with this analysis is that it confuses the idea of what a profession is at its core, its *essence*, with its external features, or its *attributes*. It's like defining a person by their hair colour. In principle at least, you don't develop a code of ethics or lobby for recognition in law in order to become a profession. *You do those things to defend the profession that you already are.*

This is really the project that Daryl Koehn took on in *The Ground of Professional Ethics* (1994). From the outset, Koehn's intention was analytical. That is, she wasn't so much interested in describing the professions by listing their attributes, like Greenwood and those following him were. This was another way of thinking. She wanted to identify the central core, the engine that drove them, the central logic.

Generally, the status of the three classical professions (law, medicine, the clergy) as professions is not disputed. There might be argument about who gets included in them, but the profession itself generally is not in question: if 'profession' means anything, it means these three. Using them, Koehn works with a long history of literature to try to discover the heart of the professions, and what makes them professions. Her philosophical technique is to test a range of candidates for the title to this central defining logic.

The first candidate might be that they are paid. The distinction here is between professionals and amateurs, or professionals and volunteers. She scotches this one fairly quickly. Boxers or hit men might be called professional, but we think that is a different animal from the one we are tracking. The clergy have often not been paid for what they do, but the clergy is still seen as a profession. And conceptually, there is a tradition that the fee is not a wage or a payment for services delivered, but a grateful contribution for the support of the professional who also needs to eat and pay the bills. Koehn cites the very old law, still current in the USA, that a lawyer may not sue for their fee (1994: 50).

The second candidate is expertise. This has a better chance. These people are good at what they do. They have trained a long time, they know their stuff, they are 'true professionals'. They can be trusted because of this expertise. Koehn isn't convinced by this either. Working with a professional requires a great deal of trust because the professional relationship often involves disclosing things that we would really prefer to keep to ourselves: unsightly growths or infected wounds, compromised behaviour, guilty consciences. How does expertise merit our trust?

At one level, expertise works. I know, or am pretty sure, that you, as a professional, can fix this problem I have, if anybody can, because of your skill and because you know your stuff. So I can trust you. But, Koehn argues, expertise has no moral compass. The human guinea pig experimenters in Hitler's concentration camps were skilled, but expertise engendered no obligation to cure the patient, or even to treat the patient with respect (Weindling 2005). This is the limitation of using *competence* as a measure of the professions or as a basis for professional training or accreditation. Sure, it is a necessary condition, but it is far from sufficient. Otherwise manipulative, pathological but skilled youth workers would be just fine.

A third candidate is the idea of contract. Professionals can be trusted because I can make a binding agreement with the professional to fix the problem I have. I pay their fee, whether directly or indirectly through the state, and they fix my problem. It is a transaction, in which I am the customer. No altruism is expected or sought: we are in this for our mutual benefit, and the professional is accountable through the contract. This doesn't work either. Following William May (1975), Koehn argues that it is difficult to contain the professional relationship within a contract because you often don't know what the outcome will be at the beginning. So how do you set out the terms of the contract? The relationship needs to be open-ended, open to discovering new things. It is much more like a journey than a transaction: some of those new things we might not like, but they are part of the journey.

May argues that the professional relationship is not a buyer/seller-like one, but more a marriage-like relationship in the for-better-or-worse sense. It is, May argues, a kind of partnership, a *covenant*, not a contract. Young people are not our customers, they are our clients. We do not provide a service, we serve.

Example

We live on the river in Glasgow, the Clyde, across from the last of the shipyards. One evening, I was home around dinner time, getting ready to go out to a meeting and there was a bit of a commotion outside. There was a girl, very drunk, in a flimsy dressing gown and bare feet in the freezing cold and on the wrong side of the railings. If she went in, and that is what she said she wanted to do, there wouldn't have been much that anyone could have done.

I have no contract with her. As a private citizen, I have a responsibility to look out the window and call the police or the ambulance, no more – the general moral obligation that anyone has for 'easy rescue' (Reiman 1990). As someone who provides youth work services, I am a trainer and researcher. No one has funded me for suicide prevention. It is outside hours and I am off duty. As a youth worker, however, my professional responsibility is to do what I can. And yes, eventually, she came back on to the path, and eventually the ambulance and the police arrived and they were doing a sterling job and I left them to it, after checking that that was what she wanted to happen. Am I a hero? No. It took a little time, but I was dressed up warm and on the right side of the railings. I was just being a youth worker. No youth worker would do any differently. Would they?

There is something else wrong with contract. The covenant of the professional relationship demands more of the client than that they simply 'receive the service'. If transformation is going to happen, it is the client who does that, not the professional. The professional may be the catalyst, but it is still the client who does the work. Or not. If it fails, Koehn suggests, it is quite proper to ask myself 'Has this particular physician failed me or have I failed my physician?' (Koehn 1994: 46). The idea of contract is wrong also because it erodes client discipline.

Having worked through a couple of other possibilities, she comes to a conclusion. The clue is in the name. *A professional is someone who professes*, who makes a profession of some kind. In other words, a vow, a pledge, a commitment. A professional is someone who commits him or herself to serve some sort of constituency, typically people in some state of vulnerability, with a particular focus to their service. This is essentially a *moral* position, an ethical commitment to serve. All the professions, she argues, are constituted in this way.

A profession is a relationship

This turns the question on its head. *A profession is defined not by a set of practices, but by a relationship*. A dentist isn't someone who fixes teeth. A dentist is someone who works with people to ensure their mouths stay healthy. The implications of this shift are very interesting indeed.

First, it means that the term 'professional' does not initially describe a state or a status. It is a relational term, like parent or partner. As a parent must have a child, so there must also be, for a professional, a client. If there is no client, there is no professional. Greenwood's list of attributes of a profession suddenly becomes very secondary indeed.

Second, the relationship is intentionally limited (Bayles 1981). These limits are in place in order to create conditions of safety within which a client can make themselves vulnerable. Typically, this is through some sort of disclosure: a client is able to tell someone about ugly, guilty, embarrassing, dangerous or broken aspects of themselves. The idea is that the opportunity for such disclosure can be the first step towards healing and transformation. When commentators talk about the importance of trust, they are talking about the process by which a client makes the decision that it is safe to be vulnerable with you.

In our work, the disclosure is often not verbal, and the intervention we take is often not verbal either (Morgan and Banks 1999). It might just be that we know about some of the circumstances that young people have to live with. We then create a kind of space within which options, alternatives, and different ways to be can emerge. Talking is important, but it doesn't mean that nothing has happened if the chat hasn't happened. We also wouldn't see young people's vulnerability as a product of any deficit in young people as such. Young people are emerging into adulthood, and there is a transformation that is going on in the teenage years, a confirmation of the self and the young person's position among their peers and in the world. This process involves some risk. Social conditions of exclusion and poverty exacerbate the risk, and distort what should be (and still is for many) an interesting, difficult, fun, liberating, celebrated process. Youth work creates spaces within which that can happen well, and walks with young people through the process of it happening.

This understanding is, I think, critical. Our profession, and others, work to create a kind of sacred circle within which we will meet a client (to use the general term), work with whoever they are, and whatever they have done, in order to create possibilities of transformation (see Chapter 16). It is a partnership within that space – a covenant, to use May's term – in which youth worker and young person work together to heal hurts, to repair damage, to grow into responsibility, and to promote new ways of being. This might include trying to change the external circumstances that prevent new ways of being, or that created the distortions in the first place. It doesn't always work, but it does often enough.

Third, the usual characteristics of a profession – codes of ethics, professional associations, training and recognition in law – are essentially strategies designed to protect the inner and outer integrity of that circle. In terms of the inner integrity, they are designed to ensure that the intimacy developed within that circle stays within its purpose: the healing, defence and transformation of the client. Sexual expression is excluded from the relationship because it exploits an intimacy which had a different pretext, and which held a promise that it would be protected from the complications and mixed motives of sexual demand (see Chapter 12). Economic intimacies, such as gifts, inheritances or exchanges are similarly excluded (see Chapter 14).

In terms of the outer integrity, the practice of confidentiality makes sure that the safety of the professional relationship is not betrayed by exposure to the outside world – even to other professionals – without the overt consent of the client (see Chapter 11). The principle of non-maleficence ('do no further harm') that appears in many professional codes of ethics takes responsibility for ensuring that the relationship does not put the client in further jeopardy (see Chapter 13).

Contrary to the view put by commentators such as Greenwood, therefore, Koehn argues that a profession is not constituted by features like codes of ethics, professional associations and university training. The profession already exists. These instruments are put in place to protect and strengthen the professional commitment that is already made.

Fourth, the relationship is not a symmetrical relationship but a relationship of service. It is in its nature other-directed. The professional is there to serve the client, not the other way round (see Chapters 15 and 17). It is not the case that we give the young person something, and they are then obliged to give something to us. They are obliged to give *nothing* to us, not even gratitude (though that is nice when it happens). They aren't even obliged to like us. Their only obligation in the transaction is to engage in developing their own ethical agency. Professional service certainly has its rewards, and some of them may come from clients, but we aren't hard done by if they don't, and clients aren't responsible for them (see Chapter 4). In particular, the professional relationship is not a commercial or contractual relationship, though contracts can sometimes be used within them (May 1975). Clients are not customers, buying a service. Service is primarily a verb, something we do, not a noun, a product we deliver.

Example

Are young people 'clients'?

We have had lots of conversations in the preparation of this book about the term 'client'. Youth workers often react to it, especially in the UK. It does depend a bit on where you live: North American, South African and most Australian youth workers seem pretty comfortable using the term. Some British youth workers hear connotations of condescension or lack of respect which they find hard to look past.

Substitutes are, however, routinely weak and ambiguous. *Constituency* is probably the best of them because it means that the youth worker is constituted by young people, that the power comes from them, and that we are accountable to them. But it doesn't recognise what is often our prior initiative in the relationship, or really describe the quality of the relationship. It also doesn't evoke the 'professional' as the other side of the relationship: the responsive term is probably something like 'delegate' or 'representative'. *Participant*, unless we develop an expanded meaning, primarily describes a relationship with the programme, not with the youth worker.

Some youth workers don't like the term because it implies an unequal power relationship, with the youth worker as expert, further disempowering young people (Walker 2002). But the relationship *is* a power relationship (see Chapter 15), and it isn't symmetrical. Good youth workers *are* expert (brilliant, in fact) at empowering people. Recognising the power imbalances means you take responsibility for your power in the relationship, and young people want us to be powerful on their behalf, knowing that that will not mean that we are oppressive or dominating.

The National Youth Agency code just uses 'young people'. But a young person is a young person irrespective of the relationship with a youth worker: the term says nothing special about the young person *in* the relationship, or what the relationship is. It doesn't allow you to distinguish between a young person you have a professional responsibility for and one you don't. The Victorian Code of Ethics (Youth Affairs Council of Victoria 2008) used '*primary concern*' and that is OK too, but has the problem of being unilateral: it is the youth worker who has the concern.

'Client' describes a relationship, a covenant, a partnership – in fact, all the things I have just been saying. And paradoxically, the relationship it describes is one in which the client has a great deal of power, and is active in pursuing the goals of the relationship and in holding their professional accountable.

I think the term needs to be rehabilitated. In itself, it is a good word. The smell of condescension isn't anything to do with the actual meaning of the word (its denotation) but the odour it has picked up from the corruptions of the professions (its connotation), particularly their temptation to elevate their own status at the expense of their client. It doesn't have that connotation everywhere: I doubt whether a billionaire businessman feels inferior when he is described as a client by his lawyers or accountants, so it isn't anything in the word itself. Sometimes, the term is seen to be limited to a particular context, such as closed-door counselling, but again, if you move outside social work and psychology into professions like law and engineering, those implications disappear. When I say that a young person is my client, that implies a whole set of obligations to that person that come from my understanding of the professional relationship: about what this is for, about whose interests are to be served, about who needs to be protected and how they need to be protected. I think that the concept deserves another go.

In this book, when I am talking about the relationship between a youth worker and the person they are working with, I will generally use the term 'young person', as youth work discourse prescribes (see Chapter 3). The equivalent relational term for 'professional', however, is 'client'. So when I talk about the youth worker *as a professional*, I will also need to talk about the young person *as a client*.

Conclusion

So is youth work a profession? At its core, the professional, as Koehn describes it across the classical professions, is constituted by a particular kind of relationship with the client. It is a relationship in which the client is to some extent vulnerable – to sickness, to accusation, to spiritual dislocation. The dimensions of their vulnerability may not be known beforehand, and so the relationship cannot be just a matter of commercial contract: it must be to some extent open-ended. In the light of their vulnerability, the client needs to be able to trust the professional to act in ways that protect them, and which do not exploit the intimacy evoked when people talk about sensitive matters or put themselves into another's hands. This trust may be based on the individual professional's reputation or recommendation from others, but more fundamentally rests on the professional's own public commitment to serve.

In these terms, youth work is clearly a profession. It is precisely a practice in which clients, at a point of vulnerability, are engaged in an intentionally limited (and therefore safe) relationship directed towards the transformation of their situation. To borrow Marx's terminology, youth work is a profession 'in itself' (it meets all the objective criteria) whether or not it is organised as a profession 'for itself' (self-conscious and aware of its identity and its obligations).

If that is so, then like other professions, youth work is grounded in its core ethical commitment, its public pledge to its client group. It is not that youth work *has* an ethics; rather, that youth work *is* an ethics. It is a practice of promoting justice, wholeness, and, if you will allow the somewhat old-fashioned language, individual and collective virtue: better people in a better world (Young 2006). But that needs filling out. Who is our client, then? What is a young person, such that we are called to work with them? What is the nature of our commitment? What are its limits? And how do we balance that against the other obligations that we have – to parents, to funding bodies, to our employers, to society in general?

Things to consider

This chapter has acknowledged the dangers of corruption that all professions (and, indeed, all organised and powerful groups of people) are prone to. In the light of that (acknowledging also that 'unprofessionalised' practitioners aren't necessarily squeaky clean either), do you think that youth workers in your region or country should be working towards setting up a professional association for youth workers? Should this include compulsory tertiary education and registration (and deregistration) processes, so that you couldn't call yourself a youth worker unless you were trained and registered?

3

YOUTH WORK AS A PROFESSION

Summary

The last chapter discussed the idea of a profession, arguing that the professions are constituted by their commitment to serve a vulnerable client group, and that a profession fundamentally describes a kind of relationship, rather than a status. I argued that on this understanding, youth work was, and couldn't not be, a profession. The point of this chapter is to try to sketch out what that means. We will need to work out a clear understanding of the young person as a client, and the nature of the commitment of service which we undertake. From this, we can start to define youth work as a professional practice. The chapter concludes with a definition of youth work as a professional relationship which engages the young person as the primary client in their social context.

Defining youth work

Defining youth work isn't easy. Ideally, a definition establishes what all youth workers have in common, and what marks them off from other professionals. Lots of things that we do, other people (such as social workers or psychologists or teachers) do as well. And there are things that some youth workers do, but other youth workers don't (such as organise camping trips). A definition needs to find those elements that are true of all youth workers and not true of anyone else, that include practice that is clearly youth work and exclude practice that isn't. And, ideally, a definition should be short and easily remembered.

The trouble is that the contexts in which we work are incredibly varied, including (among others) drug counselling, outdoors/adventure programmes, theatre, faith-based work, residential work with homeless young people, working on the street and work in schools. The problems that we engage with are just as varied, including crime, illiteracy, unemployment, refugee resettlement, school disengagement, homelessness and boredom. Our work might be specific to young people in their early teens, or their mid-20s; specific cultural groups; only young women or only young men; or young people with disabilities. Some youth workers are paid, some are unpaid volunteers.

The attempt to define youth work has a long and diverse history (Brew 1957; Ministry of Education 1960; Jeffs and Smith 1987; Sercombe 1997a; Martin

2002; National Youth Agency 2002; Walker 2002; Davies 2005; Youthlink Scotland 2005). Generally, the definitions try to catch what it is that youth workers do, who they do it with, how they do it, and why: in other words, to define the *practice*. Because our interest here is in ethics, we'll try and set out the logic of youth work *as a profession*.

Defining youth as a client group

Who youth workers do it with might be the easiest place to start. Or so one would think. We work with young people. But what is a young person? Serious question.

It just isn't good enough to take our client group naturalistically, 'just as young people' (Jeffs and Smith 1999b). The historical and sociological literature describes in great detail how the modern concept of youth has emerged historically and socially (see Gillis 1974; Kett 1977; Dyhouse 1981; Springhall 1984; Sercombe 1996; Bessant et al. 1998; Epstein 2007). Some societies don't seem to feel the need to define anybody as 'youth' or 'adolescent' (Seig 1976; Epstein 2007), and even in societies which have always had a 'youth' category, it has not always meant the same thing as it does now (Gillis 1974; Kett 1977; Dyhouse 1981; Springhall 1986). The age range embracing young people has changed, the traits attributed to young people have changed, the nature of their position and function within society has changed.

Even in the current environment, different professional groups have strikingly different conceptions of what 'youth' is about, and different languages and theories with which to describe them (Sercombe 1996). It isn't a natural category, given to us by biology or the natural world. In the contemporary world, different notions of youth compete, and different professions compete for their notion of youth to be regarded as the authoritative one (Tucker 2004). Ours is one of those professions.

The term that youth workers use of their clients is 'young people'. Again, this is not a 'natural' term. Not everyone uses it. Police, for example, almost never do, and psychologists and medical practitioners tend not to either (Sercombe 1996). It is a term that has a specific politics, that makes claims, refutes alternatives, and stakes out territory. It isn't innocent. It is engaged, operational. For example, it is an active rejection of the language of the 'adolescent' and of 'youths'. In order to understand our practice, we need to understand the broader context for the emergence of the youth category, how the category is constructed socially, and how our conception of youth as 'young people' also actively constitutes and shapes youth as an object of intervention.

This is not a process of finding out what youth 'really' is. All concepts of young people are social constructions, including the concepts young people have of themselves. The point is to look critically at the dominant frameworks that are out there, to be clear about the concepts *we* use, and to take responsibility for them, for the way that they shape our dealings with young people, and what we try to create as outcomes for and with them.

Age ranges

Core documents internationally tend to define the client pragmatically, by referring to an age range. So, for example, a New Zealand survey of youth work refers to the World Health Organisation's definitions of 'young people as aged 10–24, youth as 15–24 years, and adolescents as 10–19 years' (Martin 2006). Key UK policy documents, such as *Transforming Youth Work*, use 13–19 years as their core age range for service provision, with targeted services for some 11–13 and 19–25 year olds (Smith 2002).

This kind of definition is useful administratively, but is worthless conceptually. Ten year olds have very little in common with 25 year olds. Most 10 year olds are biologically children. Most 25 year olds in the world (notwithstanding the trend to delay parenthood in the West) are parents. And there is no material difference between a 25 year old and a 26 year old. The diversity of age ranges proposed to define youth, and the multitude of ages of majority, also indicate that this way of categorising young people is entirely arbitrary. A European survey of youth work policy documents notes that the category can begin from 7 years old and end anywhere up to 36 (Institut für Sozialarbeit und Sozialpädagogik 2007: 23).

Adolescence

The dominant conception in the professions (e.g. teaching, psychology, medicine and social work) is the notion of *adolescence*. North American youth work, or at least child and youth care, tends to be reasonably comfortable with this (Draft Committee for the International Leadership Coalition for Professional Child and Youth Care 1995) but youth workers in Britain, Australia and New Zealand generally are not.

A fuller discussion is available elsewhere (Sercombe 1996; Bessant et al. 1998; Sercombe et al. 2002; Epstein 2007). In brief, however, the idea of adolescence is based on three core concepts:

1. Adolescence is a stage of life, qualitatively different from other stages of life.
2. It is universal, programmed into all human beings.
3. It is inherently traumatic or troublesome.

The empirical truth of all three of these assumptions has been heavily challenged over decades of inquiry. The fact that the concept constructs young people in deficit, even as pathological, makes it questionable as a basis for youth work practice (Walker 2002). It is, and continues to be, the basis on which many of the practices of exclusion in law and policy are justified: if young people are qualitatively different from adults, and are particularly susceptible to trouble, they need different treatment and different models of governance. Especially, they need containment and control. While the concept of adolescence continues to shape public discourse about young people, its rejection by youth workers is well founded.

Transitions

Rejecting biological and pathological views of young people, youth workers have tended to see youth in social terms. The most common version of this is to do with transitions (Institut für Sozialarbeit und Sozialpädagogik 2007). While more complex and nuanced understandings of this process are emerging, this framework has tended to see human beings moving in a linear and one-way developmental pathway through the lifespan. The period known as 'youth' is concerned with the transition from child to adult, and along with this, the transition from dependence to independence, school to work, from the family home to a home of your own, from being someone's child to someone's parent, single to married (Havighurst and Dreyer 1975; Arnett 2002).

Initially, the concept of transitions was useful as a way of talking about the failure of social processes in the context of high youth unemployment. However, the fragmentation of the linear transition to adulthood is now so widespread that the usefulness of the concept of transition is questionable. Most of the statuses which might have once guaranteed accreditation as adult – marriage, a job, leaving home, parenthood – are now seen as unavailable, temporary, unreliable, or not really conferring adult status. Or they come much later in life: in the late 20s or 30s. Accreditation as adult now emerges vaguely and unevenly, one step forward and one step back, across a range of contexts in which the individual lives, rather than the product of a predictable and reliable set of developmental tasks. It is influenced by strategic choices made by the individual, but is also limited by circumstances that are beyond their control (Sercombe et al. 2002).

It is also difficult to see why transitions should particularly distinguish young people. Life is full of transitions, and it is a question as to whether the transitions between 12 and 25 are really more profound than between 25 and 38, 38 and 50, or 60 and 73. The notion of transitions continues to be useful, but only if understood as progressing irregularly and unevenly across a range of capacities and contexts, and towards a future which continues to be a journey, not a destination.

Youth as exclusion

Increasingly, intervention with young people has worked around the language of exclusion (Spence and Devanney 2006). In the modern context, especially in the UK, this has filtered down from the policy environment, but this thinking is also indigenous to youth work at the practice level (Sercombe 1989) and has been around theoretically since the 1970s at least (Seig 1976).

There is a broad range of psychological and anthropological evidence to demonstrate that once puberty has settled down (usually by the age of about 14–16) young people are biologically adult. The inherent capacities of young people, in terms of intelligence, reason and logical decision-making are no different from those of other adults (Melton 1983; Epstein 2007), though expression of adult capacity may be inhibited by environment and opportunity. Inexperience is an issue, of course, but this is only incidentally age-related, and in many areas young people may be more experienced than their elders, particularly in an environment of rapid social change (Benedict 1935).

The youth category is a product of the practice of *excluding* certain biologically adult members of a society from full participation in society, basically because they are judged to be 'too young'. What 'too young' generally means is that they have not yet assimilated the dominant social codes, and are therefore deemed to be 'unsafe': unsafe drivers, drinkers, tenants, financial managers, voters, and marriage partners. This is not because of any inherent lack of capacity: young people have both the physical and mental abilities necessary to make perfectly competent drivers or financial planners, and in many parts of the world, 14 year olds are doing all of these things (Epstein 2007). Young people are excluded from engaging in these roles or practices because it is *assumed* that they don't yet have the right 'attitudes'.

Example

John is 16. He works on a building site. He is strong and likes working and has a reputation as a good worker. However, he earns significantly less than the 30 year-old beside him does, even though it is the same job. He would like to apply for a job in a mine in his area, but the mine has a rule that he can't be employed if he is under 18. He pays taxes: direct taxes on his income, indirect taxes on his expenditure. He isn't eligible to vote, so has no say in how his taxes are spent.

John's family life is not ideal since his parents broke up and his mum began a new relationship. Three months ago, he moved out of home. He is working, so can afford his own flat. But real estate agents reject his application as soon as they find out his age. He is living in a supported accommodation project, but wants to be independent. Public housing could be a possibility, but waiting lists are long and he is a low priority. The authorities presume that, as a single man, he can find housing in the private market.

He has a girlfriend, Kathy. They have been going out together for a year. She is a year younger than him. For the last month, they have been having sex, although both of them know that if someone in authority finds out he could be charged with a serious offence, with permanent consequences, such as being on a sex offenders register.

From this perspective, becoming an adult is a process of accreditation. Youth is not fundamentally a *stage* that people *grow* out of. It is a *status* that they are *promoted* out of (Seig 1976). There are things that they can do to facilitate this process of promotion or accreditation, ways in which young people can signal to the society at large that they are ready for recognition as adult. But it is up to the society to recognise their status. And society can, and does, withhold accreditation in its own interest.

The very existence of the youth category is a product of exclusion. So exclusion is not accidental when it comes to young people: it is how the youth category is created. If you don't exclude this group of young adults, you don't have a youth category (Seig 1976). Hence the professional language-marker of youth work: the term 'young person' (Sercombe 1997b). A young person is primarily a person – a normal member of the human race, not some different kind of species. They just happen to be young. The rest of the drama is created by the social relations under which young people live.

Bringing concepts together

Youth is a paradox. Fundamentally adult, young people are still developmentally distinctive from older adults. Is this difference biological, or just a result of the processes of exclusion? New developments in cognitive neuroscience indicate that there are physical differences between the brains of teenagers and other adults, but also that physical brain structure and function is deeply shaped by social and environmental experience (Sercombe and Paus 2009). There are young people who can stand up as smart, as reliable, as skilled and as integrated as any other adult. There are other young people (but also no small number of 'adults') who are a long way from this. We do not yet know to what extent giving young people responsibility *creates* the change in structures and processes in the brain that the neuroscientists say happen in the teenage years. While current opinion is deeply shaped by the assumptions that researchers already have about young people, the probable answer is 'to a very great extent' (Sercombe 2009a). The maturity of young carers or young people returning from war would tend to confirm that.

Adulthood is not a destination. In fact, the term itself is deeply problematic. But there is something about 'coming to yourself' or 'coming into your own' or 'being grown up' that the term adulthood describes. Young people are emerging into this sense of identity, of agency, of feeling like their lives are their own responsibility and that they need also to take responsibility for others around them. Some young people are already there at age 14. Some aren't at 40.

It is difficult, even after all these years, to say what a young person *essentially* is (Sercombe 2009b). Biological adulthood is a *fairly* objective phenomenon, at least at the level of the capacity to reproduce. However, existential adulthood, the feeling and experience of being adult and the demonstration of adult social capacities, along with the corresponding cognitive structures, is deeply dependent on social context and opportunity.

There is an inside story and an outside story to this. There are individual, personal developmental factors at play, including genetics and the choices an individual makes. This is also a process that can be facilitated or retarded by the social and physical environment and by experiences. From puberty, young people are *emergent adults*. The process happens discontinuously across a range of capacities, is different from person to person and is, youth workers would argue, deeply dependent on opportunities for responsibility. However, that opportunity is often denied because of the perception of risk, that young people *as a social category* are not ready or will be unreliable.

These factors spiral, creating self-fulfilling prophecies. Environments that give young people opportunities for participation and responsibility find that young people participate and contribute effectively. Environments that quarantine young people from key social processes because they are unreliable or trouble-some find that they are immature, risk-prone and irresponsible (Seig 1976; Schlegel 2009). Most Western societies correspond to the latter. At a population level, this exclusion creates the youth phenomenon. In this context, we could define youth as *that emerging adult population which is excluded from partici-pation in the common wealth because of a perception of age-based risk.*

If that is youth, what is youth work?

In our own time, the scope and length of exclusion has been increasing expo-nentially. At the turn of the last century, puberty arrived later and adulthood ear-lier: the gap between biological adulthood and social adulthood was about five years. Now it is closer to 15 years. This has meant an elongation of adolescence and dependency – what Epstein calls the resulting infantilisation of young peo-ple – and increasing restriction on their movements and their fundamental human rights (Epstein 2007). Emergent adults who in any other time and place would have been parents are classified ever more rigidly as children.

But the risk of excluding a population is that it becomes not only excluded but disengaged. And a disengaged population, particularly of young men, is socially dangerous and individually destructive. Since the industrial revolution, youth work has responded to this risk, mostly by connecting with young people and trying to engage them, preferably on their own terms. Youth *policy* has responded to it mostly by being concerned with the potential for social disrup-tion. Policy and practice has met, often awkwardly, in the middle:

> 'We'll engage the young people and you might get some social order out of it', say youth workers.

> 'You improve social order, and for that we'll give you some resources to build relationships with young people' say those in power.

What 'engagement' might mean for youth work, and to what end, has varied (Smith 1999/2002). For much of youth work's history, the point has been to re-engage young people in 'decent' society: to facilitate, often uncritically, a greater conformity, to render young people docile without challenge or change to the established order. At other times, the point has been to leverage young people's disengagement in an attempt to challenge a power system based on exclusion, injustice and, ultimately, violence.

Mostly, youth work lives in the tension between these two poles. We live in a capitalist society, and capitalism is the most powerful engine for the generation of production, and wealth, that the world has ever seen. And innovation, and diversity, and indeed change itself. But what it has never generated is equality. Disproportionately, young people bear the brunt of that, especially if they live with multiple exclusions such as poverty, class, gender, race or disability. We work in the tension between helping young people survive their exclusion, often by re-engaging in social and economic processes, and confronting a system that excludes in the first place.

The aims of youth work

There are a number of documents which provide statements, often carefully worked through, of the aims of youth work (National Youth Agency 2002; Youthlink Scotland 2005; Institut für Sozialarbeit und Sozialpädagogik 2007). Again, the aims of youth work rest firmly on the conception of young people that you hold. If you think youth is about adolescence, or about transitions, that will shape your practice.

Koehn (1994) argues that any profession is constituted by its ethical commitment to serve a vulnerable population, and is driven towards a particular transformation. The purposes of youth work can then be thought through in terms of the vulnerability in young people that youth workers address, and the kind of transformation that they seek.

In terms of the vulnerability, if youth is indeed 'that emergent adult population which is excluded from participation in the common wealth because of a perception of age-based risk', then the vulnerability that creates a need and a mandate for professional intervention is the vulnerability that flows from exclusion. If youth is 'emergent adulthood', then the vulnerability is created by their lack of status, the uncertainty of their social position, and the fact that finding responsibility is dependent on being given it.

This leads to the second question – the question of the kind of transformation that youth workers seek. The 'outside story' is clear: youth workers seek a transformation in social arrangements so that young people are welcomed into full, active participation in the common wealth. The 'inside story' is about what happens in the young people that we are engaged with.

This transformation has been named in a hundred different ways in the youth work tradition: the transition from dependence to independence or interdependence; achieving positive self-esteem; self-actualisation – achieving one's full potential; social, economic, emotional (etc.) development; building confidence; participation; inclusion; achieving identity; individuation; raising consciousness. At their core, these terms are, I believe, trying to name the same thing. This is a quality in which people are able to see their lives as something belonging to them, in which they can actually decide how they are going to be, rather than be passive recipients, even victims, of a life determined by others or prescribed by circumstance. They take responsibility for those decisions, for the impact they have on others and the world around them, and indeed for the kind of person they become in making them. It is particularly significant for young people because, having emerged biologically as adult through the process of puberty, there is now the process of taking their place in the world as active, competent, full participants.

Sociologists call this quality *agency*. From a youth work perspective, this is not just the capacity to act, but to act well. It has an ethical element. We don't just want young people to grow up, but to grow up good (Young 1999, 2006). Helping a young person graduate from being a petty criminal to an accomplished professional criminal doesn't count as success. In the last century, youth workers generally held a narrow view of this as limited to committed Christian manhood or womanhood (Young 1999). The vision is broader (or perhaps deeper) than this now, but the core objective of goodness remains.

Liberal philosophies, which still dominate the West, have tended to see agency as a quality of the *individual*, thus generating terms like individuation, independence, liberty, self-determination, self-actualisation, individual sovereignty, achieving one's full potential. Youth work has never been satisfied with this. On the one hand, youth workers are intensely aware of the extent to which a person's capacity for agency can be limited (and corrupted) by poverty, oppression, family background, difference, psychological damage and other social circumstances – it is not just a question of choice. On the other hand, this quality of agency is also about a person acting *into* their social context: their relationships, their communities. A person is a person not only for themselves, but for their family, friends, partners, colleagues, community, and eventually, their children and grandchildren. It cannot, ever, be only individual. A person can be 'successful', but exploitative, uncaring, violent, selfish, or caring, supportive, considerate, generous. This is why the shape that a young person's agency takes is never ethically neutral, and why our intervention to enable or facilitate young people's agency isn't either (Young 1999).

The process of agency is also interactive and relational. It is never something that a young person achieves by themselves. This can be described as '*finding* responsibility' because responsibility is something that is *taken* by a person (as in 'taking responsibility for one's actions') but also *given* by the sets of social relations in which they live. (This includes not only governments, but friends, families, communities, *and* youth workers.) Young people cannot become responsible if no one will give them responsibility. Authorities may not do this willingly: not only does it involve surrendering power, but there are layers of myth about how young people are not capable, are too much of a risk. For youth workers, advocacy includes working to open up possibilities for taking responsibility that are currently denied to young people.

At the same time, youth workers confront the inequality and injustice of young people's situation, and work at the structural level to try to bring about change: to eliminate structural causes of exclusion, and to remedy the compounding effects of poor policy- and decision-making.

So youth workers do work with a problem, but the problem is not, in the first instance, the young people. The problem is the systems of exclusion that make it difficult for them to participate in the common wealth, in social and political processes, and to step up into the roles of citizen and adult which are their birthright. Of course, this system creates problems for young people, and exclusion can easily become disengagement. Youth workers also work with the consequences of exclusion for young people, including the violence, problematic drug use, poverty, isolation and alienation and ill health that predictably follows social disengagement.

This experience can cause spiralling cycles of damage which become self-reinforcing and self-replicating, and individual young people and groups of young people can themselves become secondary sources of violence and damage (Searle-Chaterjee 2000). But at the core, the source of this damage is structural, not personal, and it originated in the decisions of the powerful, not the decisions of young people.

Youth workers act by engaging young people in a professional relationship, in which the youth worker sees the client first as a young *person*, not as a criminal or a problem or a label or a potential adult (Jeffs and Smith 1999b; Walker 2002; Yohalem 2002). Within that relationship, the youth worker helps the young person negotiate the difficulties created by the exclusion of young people from the common wealth, including the loss of autonomy and agency that results, and to facilitate or regenerate the capacity to be actors in their own lives.

Defining youth work

Given the difficulty of defining youth work by what youth workers do, the literature has mostly constructed a definition by trying to tie down the key elements, or by prescribing the purposes of youth work practice, or both. For example, British youth work has been deeply influenced by the templates laid down in the Albemarle Report of 1960 (Davies 1999, Smith and Doyle 2002). The Report was written in the aftermath of the Second World War, with a burgeoning youth population in most of the Western world and a widespread concern about levels of delinquency. It saw youth as a time of risk, where young people could lose their way, perhaps permanently, in the transition to adulthood. Youth work was seen as an adjunct to home, school and work in facilitating that transition. The key elements captured in the Report were:

1. **Voluntary involvement.** Youth work should happen in places where young people could choose to be, and so could explore emerging adulthood in their own terms and in their own time.
2. **Association.** Youth work should use the developmental potential of association, of people coming together and learning to work together and make decisions together. Generally, this meant that the peer group was positively valued.
3. **Informal relationship.** The power of youth work is in the quality of the relationship between the youth worker and the young person. This is by no means unique. However, unlike many other professional relationships, youth work operationalises friendship-type relating styles, overtly pursuing a more equal style of relationship.
4. **Educational intention.** There was a strong existing tradition of informal and community-based education in the UK, including in youth work,

which became established as the core of youth work practice. Youth work was therefore generally attached to education departments and adopted educational discourses. It was seen as an adjunct to the school and complementary to school-based education (Spence and Devanney 2006).

While these elements are probably important everywhere, they haven't always been seen as constitutive of youth work. Youth work in the USA has been closely aligned with welfare discourses and with crime prevention, rather than educational ones, though the discourse of positive youth development has become increasingly influential (Pittman and Fleming 1991; Villarruel et al. 2002). In practice, this has been the case in Australia as well, although theoretically youth workers there have promoted advocacy as the key framework for understanding practice. European youth work has often promoted informal education as the key framework for practice, but has also had a strong emphasis on labour market programmes and facilitating the school to work transition (Institut für Sozialarbeit und Sozialpädagogik 2007).

The key problem has generally been that commentators have tried to find an *embracing* definition of youth work. It isn't difficult to talk about what youth workers do, the literature is able to do that quite articulately. The difficulty is to say what makes youth work *distinctive*: different from what parents, police, schoolteachers, commercial leisure proprietors, psychologists and sports coaches do. A good parent of teenagers, for example, will do informal education with their kids, will engage them voluntarily in that, and will be concerned about their personal and social development in the process. Other professions and role/relations probably don't do the spread of what is described in the Institut für Sozialarbeit und Sozialpädagogik's European survey, but individual youth workers or agencies don't either. Yet we know that youth work *is* distinctive. You know youth work (and youth workers) when you see it, and it doesn't look like anything else.

The alternative is to find an *analytical* definition of youth work. Echoing Koehn's method, let's forget about what youth workers *do*. What is the *ground* of what they do, the central dynamic? This is where Koehn's idea of the professional becomes useful (again!). If a profession is constituted by an ethical commitment to a client group, around a particular vulnerability, then the definition of youth work is established by a clear idea of the client, a clear idea of their vulnerability, and a clear idea of the sphere of action or intervention.

Who is the client?

It's a simple question. It has a simple answer. The client is the young person, or people, with whom the youth worker is engaged.

But the practice is not as simple as it first seems. First, youth work has a range of clients (see Chapter 15). Because youth work does not have an independent resource base, it is generally dependent on the benefaction of the state or of the wealthy. The state is therefore a stakeholder, and certainly sees itself as a client.

Youth workers generally work for organisations, and managers and boards of such organisations are certainly stakeholders as well. Then there are parents, schools, police, shopkeepers, local residents, the community at large – all of whom have a stake in our intervention with young people.

Within this range of very real obligations, the youth worker makes an active and positive choice about priority. The interests of the young person are primary, above all others. Fundamentally, **the primary client of the youth worker is the young person** with whom they engage (see Sercombe 1997a; Youth Affairs Council of Western Australia 2003). All other obligations, including those to the funding body, are secondary. Funding bodies give money to youth work organisations on this understanding. Or they should.

This places youth work in radical distinction to most other forms of engagement with young people. Most work with young people is not primarily concerned with what the young person wants to happen, but with sorting out a situation or alleviating problems or discomforts that young people might cause others. Social work, for example, youth work's closest relative, does not unambiguously engage the young person as the primary client, even if the young person is in the frame. Their responsibility is to balance the various interests of different stakeholders, and try to achieve the best resolution. Frequently, the state will be their primary client, as they take on statutory roles mandated by Acts of Parliament. This can include, for example, recommending a term of imprisonment for a young person in representations before a court.

Balancing these interests is an important role, and I'm not arguing for any kind of moral superiority for youth workers here. It is just that we take a different position. Young people need to know that someone is unambiguously acting for them, is on their side, and will not act against their interests, whatever the interests of other stakeholders. It means, for example, that youth workers can't do family mediation. Mediation requires the mediator to be neutral, and youth workers are not neutral. They may have a role in family mediation or case conferencing or restorative justice processes as an *advocate* for the young person, but not as a mediator. If you want a mediator, get a social worker.

There are some other professions who would argue that if they are working with a young person, then the young person is unambiguously their client. Lawyers, doctors and psychologists are (or should be) in this category. If a doctor is treating a young person, it should be the interests of the young person (rather than their parents, for example) that have absolute primacy.

The difference between these professions and youth workers is in their sphere of action. If youth is a function of social exclusion, then work with young people needs to take seriously this status, and to work with young people around the elements of their social context which impact on them. At the most benign level, young people have to negotiate their accreditation as adults, and to manage the consequences of their exclusion, including, for example, their containment through compulsory school attendance. The second condition of the definition is therefore that the youth worker engages the young person **in their social context**. The ethical imperative is that the exclusion of young people from the common wealth represents a fundamental injustice, and that we engage with the social context within which young people live, to do what we can to right that injustice and in the shorter term to mitigate the harm that it can cause.

The final part of the picture is that this is a **professional** relationship, in the terms that we have discussed earlier. As a committed relationship limited by the professional disciplines, ours is different from that of a parent or relative.

Conclusion

Actual practices and settings can and do vary widely, but youth workers hold in common their commitment to give priority to the interests of young people and to work not only towards the transformation of the young person in their social context, but also the transformation of that context. Thus:

A definition

Youth work is a **professional** relationship in which the young person is engaged as the **primary client** in their **social context**.

This definition holds whether the youth worker is paid or a volunteer, a student or a manager, trained or untrained, a bureaucrat or an academic. If you take up the challenge of being a youth worker, your primary client is young people, and your sphere of intervention is the social context in which they live. Training doesn't make you a youth worker. You seek training because you have committed yourself to be a youth worker and, ethically, it is your responsibility to be skilled and informed in your intervention. As a policy-maker or an academic, for as long as your research or your policy work has young people as its primary client, you remain a youth worker. The moment young people cease to be your primary client, you cease being a youth worker, even if you are working with them every day and your job title says 'youth worker'.

Things to consider

- If youth work is usually funded by governments or 'adult' organisations that have their own objectives in the work, how realistic is it for youth workers to claim that the young person is *ever*, in principle, their primary client? Isn't this just aspirational, and doesn't it set youth workers up?
- Can the idea of the 'client' ever be redeemed from its connotations of condescension and helplessness? Can you think of an alternative?
- In the work that you do, what concept of 'youth' is being used?

4

MOTIVATIONS

Summary

Ethics and motivations are caught up in each other. Ethics calls for, and drives towards, response. Our motivations will shape our ethics, both individually and as a profession, and, hopefully, our ethics will also shape our motivations, calling them into question and to account when they need to. This chapter examines what our motivations are and what legitimate rewards might be, not only for each of us as individuals, but as members of the profession. Because so much youth work is done within a faith-based context, there is also a special discussion of religious motivations for practice.

Youth work sits in an interesting position with respect to the relationship with young people as the client. Unlike most professions, the professional relationship in youth work isn't initiated, in most cases, by the young person. Young people may not perceive they have any need for a youth worker. On what basis do we pursue a relationship with young people (as we most definitely do)? What right do we have to interfere in people's lives? What is our mandate? And what are our motivations? Or at least, what are legitimate motivations?

There is no question that some motivations flow from our understanding of youth, and of youth work, as we explored in the last chapter. Koehn argues that the kind of knowledge that is developed in the professions is not neutral, objective expertise, but a committed engagement with the object of their work – what the ancients called *scientia*, 'a passion or perfection arising from the union of something intelligible and an intellectual power' (Koehn 1994: 20). The object's own character guides the inquiry and the form it takes; the good to be pursued is present in the inquiry.

So the nature of youth determines the nature of youth work. If youth is created as a population group by its exclusion from the common wealth, and if youth work is about addressing that exclusion and mitigating its damage, then there is a moral claim for justice which motivates our profession. For many of us, the motivation to work with young people comes from the frustration of seeing the way that young people are pressed into lives that are less than they could be, of the waste of talent and capacity involved, and for the way that not only young people, but we as a society are the poorer for that. When we express our motivations collectively, as a profession, it tends to be with this kind of intent, though not necessarily in these words.

But we also have our own motivations. We want to be financially secure. We want to be loved. We want to be respected. We want to help. We want to feel good about the society we live in. We want social recognition. We want to have fun. We want to keep learning, be stimulated. We want other people to be able to have those things too. We want to belong. We want to feel safe. We want to become more like the person we want to be. We might want to be rich and famous, though youth work seems an odd choice if that's at the top of the list.

All of those motives are fine. Any one of them can result in seriously disordered practice if they get out of balance. Professional discipline is significantly about keeping the multitude of our motivations in their proper place. Part of that is knowing ourselves well enough to know what our motivations are. Another is about knowing where our different motivations belong, and which are about me, and which are about the interests of the young person.

Other-directedness

The peculiar characteristics of a profession as distinguished from other occupations, I take to be these:

First. A profession is an occupation for which the necessary preliminary training is intellectual in character, involving knowledge and to some extent learning, as distinguished from mere skill.

Second. It is an occupation which is pursued largely for others and not merely for one's self.

Third. It is an occupation in which the amount of financial return is not the accepted measure of success.

(Brandeis 1914: 2)

So wrote Judge Brandeis in an address to open a new college – actually, a business college – in 1912. His argument was for business to embrace the ethical aspects of their work, especially the requirements of justice for their workers, and take their place among the professions. In doing so he laid down a template for a profession, as Koehn does, in terms of its ethics, and especially in terms of its motivations. Whether business was a good candidate for that, I'm not sure, but that is another question. Brandeis' core argument is that a profession is distinguished by being *other-directed*. In other words, it isn't about you. Your youth work is about the young people you work with. As the previous chapter argued, *they* are your primary client, not you.

This characteristic used to be understood in terms of *altruism*, but this has become more difficult as a concept largely because the meaning of the word has itself moved. Originally, it meant activity that was directed primarily towards the interests of others. Over time, the term has hardened to mean activity in which any self-interest is absent. In doing so, it has lost its usefulness for our purposes. Aside from the question of whether anyone ever does anything in the complete absence of a personal motive, Koehn argues that altruism is, in the long term, unstable. I might be prepared to do all sorts of things for you without any reward, but after a while, that is going to be very annoying and I'm going to resent it. And probably start doing things badly, even vindictively. Practice becomes sound when it is 'shown not only to benefit the client but necessarily and intrinsically to satisfy the professional' (Koehn 1994: 119–20).

Our practice is other-directed, but not altruistic. Our work is directed towards the service of young people, but we have our own motivations. How does that work? What are our rewards in the youth work relationship? How do we find the balance?

Koehn describes the rewards of professional practice in two ways. First, she argues that the professional shares in the good that they are pursuing for their client. There is, she says, the 'physician's share of health' and the 'lawyer's share of justice' (1994: 123). So, as we facilitate young people's development, we facilitate our own. As we seek justice and inclusion for them, we make ourselves more just and inclusive. As we help young people learn, we learn. As we create environments that are open and accepting and developmental and fun, we are accepted and develop and become more open and fun.

Second, she argues that the act of professing, of taking on the profession, has a motive beyond the service which it provides to the client. It might be obvious that *someone* needs to engage young people if they are being excluded. But why should it be me?

The language she uses for this comes from the classics and might sound a bit high-minded, but that's OK. The motive for the professional, she argues, is the motive of self-perfection. This comes not as the *object* of our work. There is a long tradition that one cannot find perfection (or happiness, or a number of other good things) by seeking it directly. As John Lennon said, life is what happens while you are busy making other plans. If we try merely to become more perfect, more good (and so much more if we think we have succeeded), the great risk is that we become self-righteous and pretentious and, frankly, insufferable. It is in the process of *service*, in the process of being *other*-directed, that we become better people, better versions of ourselves.

At some level, I think we know that about our practice, although I don't think I was conscious of it until Koehn pointed it out. But from the beginning I liked what youth work was doing to me. I liked the kind of person it was making me, even as it confronted me with my limitations and inadequacies. Or maybe because it confronted me with those things. And having been insulated from many of the injustices of society all my life up until then, at least then I knew about some of them close up. I knew good and evil. I might not be able to do much about those injustices, but I wasn't just someone standing by.

For Koehn, then, the key motivation for the professional is:

the pursuit of self-perfection through the service of the client.

Now, I'm not claiming anything about purity of motives here. The long list of motivations at the beginning of this chapter don't suddenly disappear because we recognise a more transcendent motive about becoming a better person, or self-perfection, or virtue, or whatever else you want to call it – the 'what kind of person do I want to be?' question. But these other motivations – the desire to earn good money, to be recognised, to be loved, to have fun, to feel safe – are put in context and ordered by this primary other-directedness. As much as I might want these things, and be motivated by them, this practice is not about me. It is about this young person that I am talking to, or this group of young people that I'm planning this event with. These other things have their place, I might still need to attend to them, and there may be a time when I need to give them some priority, but they are not why I do youth work.

There is a family of motivations, however, that require some further examination, not because they aren't other-directed, nor because they aren't concerned with self-perfection through the service of young people. They do, however, confront the question of what youth work is for.

Youth work and proselytising

The history of youth work in most Western countries began with evangelism, with the imperative to introduce young people to the Christian faith. For that matter, the histories of many individual youth workers began with evangelism, with youth work as a process of 'seeking the lost'. In some traditions, this was the only focus of interest. The analysis was that the primary need of young people was spiritual, the primary transformation a religious conversion, and that the transformation of a young person's material life would naturally follow the renunciation of alcohol and other drugs, unprincipled sexual activity, crime, fighting and the rest of the deadly sins. These pursuits would be replaced by sobriety, hard work, contribution to the community and usually (though by no means always) political conservatism.

Many people whose motivations began with evangelism began to notice more and more the difficulty of these young people's lives, and the often routine injustice that filled them. To be sure, their lives would often get better with the moral focus of religious commitment and the support of religious communities, but the thing was, things should never have been like that in the first place. Rich people needed God no less, but somehow crime, unemployment, ignorance, poverty and alcoholism didn't seem to be as inevitable a consequence of a godless but affluent existence.

So the analysis tended to move on to understand the conditions of injustice and deprivation that shape the lives of young people like this. Without totally discarding theology as an explanatory schema, youth work moved on to political and sociological analysis to understand the position that young people were in. The move away from theological justifications for intervention was accelerated by partnerships with the state, where doctrines of the separation of church and state generally required government-supported youth work to be secular, at least on the surface.

The first motivations of youth work, then, were religious. These motivations no longer dominate the field, at least not overtly. But religious motivations continue to be active among youth workers, and faith-based organisations like the Salvation Army, the YMCA and Barnardo's are big players in the field, as well as the welfare/care/youth work wings of the major denominations, Islamic and Jewish organisations and other religious groups. No book about youth work ethics would do its job without giving serious attention to faith-based traditions within youth work, and proselytising as a primary motivation for youth work practice.

So can work with religious intent be youth work?

The short answer is yes, it can. But not all work with young people done from a faith perspective is youth work.

Will the definition of youth work help?

This is a reasonable test case for the definition of youth work that we encountered in the last chapter. Faith-based youth work is youth work if it engages the young person in a professional relationship as the primary client, in their social context.

First, it isn't youth work if the relationship isn't a professional one. Many church-based youth groups work on friendship and peer-based networks, and the language for the facilitative role reflects that: 'youth leader' rather than 'youth worker'. The professional disciplines are not presumed to apply, and don't. There isn't a problem if a youth leader forms a sexual attachment to another member of the youth group.

Second, it isn't youth work if the young person isn't the primary client. The work needs to be driven by the young person's situation and, significantly, to be on their terms. If the motivation for service is the faith community's ambitions for growth or for the status attaching to conversion, or a programme of containment to make sure that the young people don't stray from the faith irrespective of their own reasonable but different choices, it isn't youth work. If service is withdrawn when a young person declines conversion or leaves a faith community, there is clearly also a problem. If a young person has no interest in the faith question, but is continually confronted with it anyway, it is again difficult to see how they are the client. If formal religious instruction is a condition for access to more attractive parts of the programme, that is a problem too.

Being the client means more than that the work is in the young person's interest (as we perceive it). It means that the work is centred on the young person, especially their perceptions, needs and purposes. So it isn't enough that we think that what we are planning would be good for them.

Third, it isn't youth work if the youth worker doesn't engage the young person in their social context. If the concern is only or even primarily with ultimate questions, on the person's spiritual life and on their religious commitments, it isn't youth work. Maybe here, 'youth ministry' is a more honest term.

It is a question of being clear about the scope of your professional practice. A cognitive psychologist might be at the top of their field, but they don't do brain surgery, even though brains might be especially what they are interested in, and mostly what they work on. It is absolutely legitimate for a young person's spiritual life to be one of the questions that we pursue in the youth work encounter: not to tell them ours or to tell them what theirs should be (because youth work is not about telling), but to listen, to assess, to clarify, to contribute and, if required, to refer. The state of a young person's connection to their spiritual tradition or community of faith is part of their social context, and as important as their connection to school and to family. This is so especially if a young person engages me as their youth worker knowing that I am working for a faith organisation. And if I am working for a faith organisation, they should know.

Conclusion

In youth work, as in life, our practice is shaped by our motivations. We are used to these being expressed in terms of the aims or goals of whatever project we happen to be working on, and sometimes, the goals or purposes of youth work more generally. For example, the National Youth Agency's foundational document, *Ethical Conduct in Youth Work*, says:

> The purpose of youth work is to facilitate and support young people's growth through dependence to interdependence, by encouraging their personal and social development and enabling them to have a voice, influence and place in their communities and society.

> (National Youth Agency 2002: 3)

The purposes of our practice derive directly from our analysis of what constitutes the problem with respect to young people. I have argued that the obligation to intervene arises from the exclusion of young people and our consciousness not only of the fundamental injustice of that exclusion but the damage and waste that it causes. The National Youth Agency's statement of purposes is congruent with this. The analysis here, I think, is that what ought to be a fluid, natural and celebrated transition from dependence to interdependence (or, as we have described it elsewhere, ethical agency) becomes problematic because of young people's exclusion (the absence of 'voice, influence and place in their communities and society' (National Youth Agency 2002) and that this inhibits their social and personal development.

There are always a number of motivations, both externally and internally, principled and practical. We need to keep funding bodies satisfied, to meet expectations of our communities, to keep our jobs. We need to be loved and accepted, to be safe and secure, to be stimulated and to learn, to feel like we are moving and making progress.

These various motivations are ordered by our core understanding of what our profession involves: in this case, the principle of the young person as the primary client, the field of practice as the young person in their social context, the purpose of their emancipation from exclusion and infantilisation into productive, responsible, ethical, critically engaged, committed and respected members of their societies.

Our personal motivations are ordered by the core purpose that we share with every true professional: to pursue self-perfection through the service of the other. As young people find life through our work, so do we.

Things to consider

- Isn't this talk of self-perfection a bit pretentious? Isn't it just a job, and you do it the best you can? Is there anything wrong will doing youth work just to pay the bills?
- Is political or philosophical proselytising any different from religious proselytising? For example, feminist consciousness-raising? Or socialist organising? Or trying to sign young people up to the environmental movement?
- If you did lead a young person through a religious conversion, what are your obligations to them then? Are these consistent with your youth work?

Part Two

Method and Theory in Ethics

5

THINKING ETHICALLY

Summary

This part of the book aims to provide practical tools for thinking ethically. This chapter lays out a core problem that we have in working together: the apparent lack of a consensus on what is right and wrong, and the lack of any kind of foundation on which a consensus might be based. However, that doesn't mean that ethical thinking can no longer be done, or that it is no longer possible to work together ethically.

The discipline of thinking ethically is no longer simple, if it ever was. The contemporary world is a pluralist world. Examples of different ways of living ethically confront us from other parts of the world, from other societies, and from different communities within our own society. In such an environment, it is harder to be clear about the boundaries of ethical action, about ways to be good to each other, about patterns of behaviour that can be relied on. We also live in a *postmodern* world, where, it is argued, the claims of external authorities of all kinds have collapsed (Bauman 1992), including not only organised religion and tradition, but also science and even rationality itself. This may not be true for individual people, but outside a single-ideology environment it is hard to find a common basis for ethical action. Paradoxically, this is precisely the kind of environment where it is ever more important to be clear about the principles under which we dare to intervene in the lives of young people and to act on their behalf.

Postmodernism and the ethics environment

There are lots of descriptions about what the postmodern condition is, and about how it might work out in different fields. As I see it, there are two central and related features of the postmodern condition. They are (1) the collapse of authorities, and (2) the rejection of essences.

The rejection of essences means that you can't establish that there is such a thing as 'reality' independent of the symbol-systems in your head. Plato thought that somewhere, there must be a true and reliable and *essential* idea of what justice, or loyalty, or compassion, or virtue is, and it is the duty of the philosopher to find it and communicate it. Postmodernists suggest that such notions are not fixed, that there is no black book somewhere in the fabric of the universe where all these things are defined and fixed in stone, but that all meanings are negotiated, that all meanings flow out of social discourse and cannot be fixed or really even found. There is no 'essential' meaning of the term 'justice'. Indeed, there is no such thing as justice independent of the way that people generate the concept. 'Justice' is a symbol of a certain way of living together, or doing relationships, or of judging the fairness of events or situations, and it changes and fluctuates and is seen differently by different people in different places.

The collapse of authorities doesn't only mean that postmodernity rejects existing authorities. There is nothing new in that. In the West, up until the nineteenth century, ethics had usually been tied to the authority of God. As modernity challenged the pre-modern world (from about the seventeenth century on), it challenged also the basis for pre-modern ethics. For the moralists of the Enlightenment, the authority of the idea of God had been cast off, and human beings were now free to seek a more rational basis for the ethical life. This established a new authority for ethics, different from the pronouncements of God as heard through the mouths of the priests: the rule of Reason and of the scientific method.

Commentators on postmodernity argue that in the postmodern world, even this authority has fragmented and broken down. It may be that science has proven a particular act to be harmful. But so what? In the postmodern world, this is no reason for acting or not acting. People still smoke, and still take up smoking. Reason has lost its authority too.

In the postmodern world, we are frequently aware of how Reason can be a mask for particular interests. In the irrationality of food surpluses amid Third World famine, all impeccably justified on rational ethical grounds, children still starve. Because we are exposed to a huge diversity of human cultures through travel, the communications revolution and the media, we are familiar too with how relative authorities and customs and rules are, and how alien codes of behaviour have their own logic. In the face of this, it is not clear that the 'irrationality' of emotion or desire should not be just as good a basis for ethical action as Reason. Not that emotion or desire or even madness are now the new authorities. In the postmodern world there can be no authorities. The authorities have all collapsed (Baudrillard 1983).

Postmodernity doesn't mean that a decision to align oneself with a way of thinking about ethics is not possible (though some would dispute this). On the contrary, in order for us to live and work together, it becomes even more necessary. But there aren't any authorities that can command universal assent, that are able to style their pronouncements as absolute truth and expect everyone to comply – even the authority of Reason. In this context, using Bauman's (1992) term, ethics becomes a bit more tribal.

Making ethical judgements and judging

So what now is the *basis* for ethics? How is it that human beings act ethically at all? And what is the basis for agreement about what is wrong and right, if there is any agreement worth speaking of? Is it that God has decreed how people should live, and will ultimately reward those who live well and punish those who live exploitatively or corruptly? More passively, is it in our nature, in the way God made us or in the way the evolutionary process has shaped us genetically? Or is it Reason, informed by careful observation and the collection of data, and informing appropriate action? Or the laws of karma, or the community of our higher selves? Or simply the rules of our social and economic system, generated by the system and imparted through the processes of socialisation? Is it just by agreement, that human beings contract together to obey certain rules?

This is one of the questions that ethics as a discipline struggles with. Because it is about competing authorities, lots of argument goes on about it. The difference between the ethical systems in the next chapter is usually a function of difference in this basis of authority. For youth workers who are trying to work with people who have often been treated badly, and trying to get it right, it is not just an academic question, but a question also of where our own commitment lies (Bauman 1992).

Things to consider

- So where is all this leading? Do we no longer know what is right and wrong? Is it now impossible to make judgements about the actions of others, and for them to make judgements about our actions?
- Does ethics all depend on accidents of birth, what kind of family you were brought up in, what nation or cultural group, what economic situation, what period of history?
- Dostoevsky said that if God is dead, everything is permitted. Is the idea of God now dead? Is, indeed, everything permitted?
- Is there nothing that we can say that is absolutely wrong, no matter what the circumstance?

Absolutism and relativism

The branch of ethics which traditionally sought to define these things is generally known as *metaethics*. In the contemporary context, rather than give absolute definitions, a more realistic project might be to try to be clear about the meaning of terms when we use them, and to try to use them consistently. Or at least to be aware when the ground is shifting.

The position that says that no ethical meanings can be established is known as *nihilism*. The position that says that there are no universal ethical norms but that there are still valid principles based on one's culture and circumstance is known as *relativism*. The position that says that regardless of what a person or culture believes, there are universal ethical requirements is known as ethical *absolutism*.

The standard position in most of the human services is relativism. As youth workers, we continually confront difference between our own ethics and those of the people we work with: about property, about sex, about drug use, about the care of children, about how outsiders should be treated. It makes sense to look at how different cultures have generated different ethical systems and how they work, and to refrain from imposing our own judgements on the situation. But there is an easy relativism, where we just tolerate everything and challenge nothing, and probably avoid potentially conflicting situations, and a more principled relativism which struggles with the facts of working with cultures (or the organisation that we work for!) where the ethics seem fundamentally askew. And they can be. To say that a belief or a practice is cultural doesn't mean that it isn't wrong. Cultures as well as individuals can become corrupt. Slavery was culturally acceptable in the eighteenth century.

Example 1

Mary Midgley, in 'Trying out one's new sword' (1993b), discusses the samurai tradition, in which a new sword must be blooded by going to the nearest crossroads, and beheading the first person who comes along in a single blow. Her position is that while this is a very ancient tradition, it is just wrong. What do you think?

Example 2

There are youth workers who will be working in male subcultures (e.g. outlaw biker cultures or certain street gangs) where rape, under certain circumstances, is seen as perfectly legitimate behaviour. If a woman places herself in a position where she is accessible to the group, for example by going back to their space with them, and especially if she is drunk, then the question of whether she wants to have sex, or with whom, no longer arises. Whoever wants to have sex with her will.

Can this be anything other than rape? And is rape anywhere, ever, morally justifiable behaviour? If it isn't, doesn't that mean that the ethic of sexual autonomy over one's own body, at least, is absolute? And if that ethic is absolute, is it the only one?

If relativism is sometimes seen as a cop-out, absolutism is often seen as arrogant. Like saying: 'I believe that I have the truth and therefore, if you have a different stance, you are mistaken.' But there is also a more *dialogic* absolutism, which might believe that there are absolute values but that my understanding or appreciation of them is likely to be imperfect, especially given my inclination to self-interest and my potential for self-deception and rationalisation. And that anyway the standards are likely to play out differently in different circumstances. So while I might have an immediate reaction to behaviour that seems wrong to me, I am committed to dialogue, to talk about it, to try together to work out an understanding of where the truth lies.

These questions are especially relevant in youth work. Frequently, we are working across cultures. Different cultures frequently express different moral stances about things like sex and relationships, about attitudes to property (including not only theft but also ownership and sharing), about attitudes to authority, about loyalty and respect for tradition. How are we to deal ethically with this range of values?

Example 3

A key principle often promoted in basic youth work training is the principle of non-judgemental practice, influenced largely by the Carl Rogers approach to counselling. Carl Rogers (1961) advocated a stance of *unconditional positive regard*, so that no matter what kind of person you were working with, or what they had done, it was necessary to convey a warm positive regard for the person and not to stand in judgement of them or their actions. Non-judgementalism still stands as a core principle in most community work. Closely aligned with this is the principle that it is wrong for workers to impose their values on the young people with whom they work.

But consider a situation in which you are working with a young woman who is repeatedly beaten up by her boyfriend. You are also working with her boyfriend. Can you avoid judging him – and should you? Is it right to allow actions which are blatantly exploitative to pass without comment? Is it not only allowable, but obligatory, to name violence and injustice for what it is? Can tolerance go too far? By refusing to moralise, are we perpetuating wrongs?

Making moral judgements

In *Can't We Make Moral Judgements?* (1993a), Mary Midgley argues that the popular prohibition on moral judgement is inconsistent and not very helpful. Principles like respect for another's property, benevolence and so on are often shared. This is what makes it possible to understand the cultural practices of others, and to make intelligent cross-cultural comment about moral practices. The other point is that people often make statements which indicate a non-mainstream morality, but which are really justifications for unethical behaviour. For example, when a person justifies their sexual adventurism by criticising an outmoded morality, but gets very upset when someone else sleeps with their boyfriend or girlfriend. Or when a thief is outraged at their goods being stolen.

Martin Buber (1965) argues that guilt is something real which needs to be addressed, and in order for it to be addressed, moral judgements must first be made. He describes an example of a young woman of his acquaintance who is helped by her therapist to deal with a guilty conscience so that it no longer gave her trouble. In the process, rather than healing her, capacities which she had previously were destroyed, and she was, according to Buber, permanently ethically damaged. Rather, Buber says, what is required is that I recognise my wrong-doing, recognise myself in my wrongdoing (and so the need for me to change), and undertake to make whatever compensations or reparations are possible or appropriate to the person I have injured.

Kerry Young (2006) suggests that the practice of youth work is precisely about producing a more moral situation, a situation in which violence is not done to young people, and in which young people do not do violence to others. This kind of practice necessitates making moral judgements, and of assuming the right to intervene in situations in order to influence outcomes, and to intervene in relationships to reduce levels of exploitation and oppression. Anti-oppressive work, whether around sexism, heterosexism, racism or more micro situations such as bullying, all involve making ethical judgements and demonstrating a willingness to intervene.

At the same time, there *is* something objectionable in what is normally called moralising or judgementalism. Judgementalism generally refers not to the practice of making ethical judgements, but of making judgements in ignorance, in haste, in arrogance, and without due recognition of our own ethical blind spots, or of making judgements not in order to heal situations but to offer an opportunity for us to claim moral superiority and diminish or condemn the other.

On the other side, a refusal to judge or to intervene may deny young people the very thing that they need most from us at particular points. The young man who beats his girlfriend *needs* to know that it is not OK, and to look closely at the mechanisms through which he allows himself recourse to this kind of action. While he needs to be understood, and to understand the roots of his action, he does not need to be excused. This needs to be done sensitively and skilfully, and it may be wise to work slowly on things (depending on the issue) rather than jump in and reduce the chance of change. But that is a strategic matter, a matter of what mode of intervention will work best, rather than a denial of the principle.

Perhaps more importantly, we have an obligation to intervene when our colleagues are acting unethically, and they have the same obligation to us. Part of the point of this kind of ethical conversation is to come to some agreement about what the important ethical principles are in our engagement with young people. So while we have our own personal ethics in our practice (and there is no substitute for that), we are involved also in a community of practice that names itself 'youth work' and whose name we share. As we accept the identity and the benefits of youth work, we also accept its disciplines.

Conclusion

In the postmodern world, according to Zygmunt Bauman (1992), our personal ethics can no longer be compelled by external authorities. Nothing is compelling. The truth of our ethics is established by our own commitment.

As youth workers, we judge the exclusion of young people to be wrong by our shared commitment to what a society should be, and indeed our society's own claims to be a democracy. The same is true for other examples that we have talked about – the violence of young men, the tolerance of high levels of unemployment, the practices of racism. Even human rights can have no authority outside the commitment of persons, associations and states to the core values about human life and human society that are embodied in them. Is it possible to prove objectively that young people should not be excluded? Probably not. But that is our commitment, and youth workers work hard to address exclusion where they see it.

So when a difference of opinion about ethics arises (as it often does), there can no longer be an appeal to authority, unless we agree on the authority – as might be the case, for example, in faith-based work, or human rights-based work, or when we have agreed to a code of ethics. In most cases, what is needed is a process of *dialogue*: a process where I deeply listen to you and your way of seeing the world, and try as openly and honestly as I can to communicate my own (Bauman 1992; Koehn 1994). If we can find common ground (and this is more often the case than not), then perhaps we can try to work towards a position that is consistent and reflects the values we share and to which we are committed. At their best, moral codes, including codes of ethics, are the product of a long process of that dialogue.

However, different people do have different ways of going about it. The next chapter explores a range of different ethical theories, which give rise to different methods for making ethical decisions. In the process, we'll try to see if we can make them talk to each other.

6

ETHICAL THEORY

Summary

As the last chapter indicated, there are a range of frameworks for thinking ethically. This chapter provides an overview of some of the key approaches to deciding whether an action is ethical or not. Each of them has its own strengths and weaknesses, and the chapter concludes with the possibility of using different frameworks depending on what the situation demands.

Ethical ideas have generally been grouped into three broad families: *consequentialist* (or teleological) theories, *deontological* theories, and *virtue*-based theories. There is a wide variety of conceptions within these groupings, of course, and other frameworks which don't fit easily into any of them, but this might help us get some perspective on the field at least.

Briefly, consequentialist theorists think that whether an action is ethical depends on the consequences of the action. If an action produces good consequences (on balance), it is a good act and is morally sound. If an action produces harmful consequences (on balance), it is a bad act and ought not to be pursued.

Deontological frameworks, on the other hand, are concerned with the inherent rightness or wrongness of the act, regardless of the consequences. The term comes from the Greek *deos* (= duty): the focus is on the act itself. Telling a lie is wrong because it is wrong, not because of any bad results, and would still be wrong if good resulted.

Virtue-based ethics focus not so much on inherent moral qualities of the act as on the kind of person that you want to become, and the kind of person that acting in a particular way will tend to make you. More broadly, virtue-based ethics also looks at the kind of society in which you want to live and in which to bring up your kids, and urges people to make ethical choices consistent with those values. What you want others to be like will influence the way you treat other people too.

Consequentialist ethics

Utilitarian approaches, in one form or another, form the philosophical base of most social policy and the rationale for many methods of practice in youth work. Certainly, the idea that we should do what is best for the communities in which we live has a lot going for it. *Utilitarianism*, in its various forms, is the classical example of this, but *ethical egoism* and *Marxist ethics* would generally be consequentialist as well.

Utilitarianism

The classical statement of utilitarianism was laid down by Jeremy Bentham in 1789. Bentham wanted to derive ethical thinking from first principles: indeed, from Nature itself.

> Nature has placed mankind under the governance of two sovereign masters, *pain* and *pleasure*. It is for them alone to point out what we ought to do…
>
> (quoted in Sommers and Sommers 1985: 103)

Bentham calls this *the principle of utility*. Utility is pretty much anything that you want or can use, anything that makes you feel good. That might be a silly hat for a birthday party, or it might be working in an orphanage in Africa, or it might be something that stops you feeling pain, such as a warm coat (even if you don't particularly like the coat). He doesn't make a value judgement about one against the other: a silly hat is not, in itself, inferior to an orphanage in Africa, though there may be elements that make you decide that the latter is more pleasurable. Moral action, for Bentham, involves working out what is going to bring most pleasure or avoid most pain. It isn't just an individual thing. Our actions also affect others, so we need also to calculate the effect of our actions. So it isn't just what feels good to me, but '*the greatest good for the greatest number*'.

How do you work that out? It isn't just a question of what feels good at this moment. According to Bentham, there are a number of criteria which might mean that you choose an activity that might not be that pleasurable in the short term (cleaning your house, for example, or staying home and studying) but which will work out to generate greater pleasures in the long term (Sommers and Sommers 1985).

In principle, one ought to be able to work out the balance of pleasure and pain deriving from a given action, and therefore whether that action ought to be pursued.

This perspective has a number of strengths. On the surface, it doesn't depend on people sharing an ideology, except the belief that pleasure is good and pain is bad. For that reason it has been really useful in the negotiation of ethical conflict or partnership working. In this case, utilitarianism's appeal to an objective weighing of the costs and benefits to everyone concerned, regardless of traditional sensibilities about the issue, is attractive. It has been especially influential in the development of social policy. There are some difficulties though.

First, the consequentialist approach sometimes gives results which don't seem quite right. An action might be OK on calculation of pains and pleasures, but seems intuitively wrong.

Example 1

In 2003, Armin Meiwes advertised on the internet for a volunteer who was willing to be killed and eaten, and another man, Bernd-Jürgen Brandes, answered the advertisement. The two men met, and Meiwes cut off Brandes' penis, cooked it and they ate it together. Then Meiwes stabbed Brandes, cut him up, cooked and ate some of him, froze some and buried the rest (Guardian 2003). On the surface of it, from a utilitarian point of view, this is fine, if a little weird. But it feels wrong, doesn't it?

Example 2

'The ones who walk away from Omelas' is a classic short story written by Ursula Le Guin in 1974 (it is available in a number of places on the internet if you want to read it, but also is excerpted in Sommers and Sommers 1985). The story explores a hypothetical utopian city: educated, prosperous, liberal. For reasons that no one really understands, this prosperity and quality of life is conditional on the imprisonment, under the harshest of conditions, of a small child. Despite the unequalled quality of life in Omelas, every year, a number of citizens 'walk away from Omelas', unable to live with the actual ethical reality of the greatest good of the greatest number. Doesn't this indicate a problem with consequentialist ethics?

Second, the scope of ethics is very broad. In principle, all acts are ethical acts because all acts have the potential to generate pleasures or pains, however minor. At the moment, I am about to make myself a cup of coffee. But I know that the circumstances of the coffee trade are deeply unethical. Coffee is grown in third world countries, often at the expense of food production, in order to earn foreign currency. The primary need for foreign currency in many of these countries is the purchase of military hardware, often used to oppress the very people who are growing the coffee. My action is supporting the coffee trade.

Now, I can still probably justify my cup of coffee. (I would really like a cup of coffee, and it probably won't contribute much to the coffee trade one way or another.) But do I want to? Do I want to have to work out the ethics of every action in my day, from getting up in the morning, to what I have for dinner, or what I watch on television?

In order to counter this problem, some philosophers have suggested that very few situations are unique, and an assessment of the consequences in standard cases might be used then to establish a rule for that case (similar to the way that most laws are framed, or the rules for a youth centre, or policies for an agency). So adultery is immoral because the standard consequence of adultery is painful, despite the short-term pleasure. This is known as *rule utilitarianism*, as opposed to *act utilitarianism*.

This might work. The problem with it is that while I can see why I shouldn't do things that cause pain, it is harder for me to see why I shouldn't do things that have caused pain on other occasions, but which I don't think will cause pain on this one. Rule utilitarianism might be a pragmatic short-cut, but whether it can command my conscience is another matter (Smart 1973).

Third, the theory ignores the reality that the calculation needs to be done by people. People have interests: they see their own pains and pleasures clearly and vividly, and those of others rather less clearly and vividly. The amount of power that people have for their voices to be heard concerning their pains and pleasures varies. It is hard to conceive of a society in utilitarian terms where the interests of the powerful do not determine the morality of the society.

Fourth, the actual pragmatics of the calculation are hard to imagine, especially once one gets beyond the micro. The same event does not have regular effects. Some people are profoundly distressed when people steal from them. Others get annoyed but it doesn't really bother them that much. Physical violence is life-destroying for some people. For others, it is a fairly routine occurrence and not a big deal: in fact, they often seek it out. How on earth does one manage the calculation, even across a neighbourhood, let alone a city?

Notwithstanding these difficulties, utilitarianism has been powerful, especially in framing public policy. In health, for example, policy-makers have to make decisions about the availability of certain subsidised drugs, measuring the benefits against the costs. Decisions are made about the location of youth services based on the relative advantage to young people from poor backgrounds versus wealthier ones. It is difficult to see how things can be different at that level, but because of the limitations of utilitarianism, practitioners need to be watchful of public policy and draw attention when the calculation is biased in favour of the powerful, or when seemingly immoral decisions (e.g. those that contravene basic human rights) are made on the basis of utilitarian arguments.

Ethical egoism

Ethical egoism has a long history, going back at least to Plato's *Republic* (about 360BCE). In the modern period, Thomas Hobbes' *Leviathan*, written in the seventeenth century, and Adam Smith's *Wealth of Nations* (in the eighteenth century) took this line. In the standard simplification of this work, Smith thought that everybody's best interests would be served if each individual person followed their own individual interest. Progress and prosperity would emerge for the society as a whole from the cumulative effects of everybody's egoistic action, like a kind of divine hand guiding the society (the so-called 'invisible hand' theory). More recently, it is identified with the work of Ayn Rand (1997; Rand and Branden 1964) and in some strands of new-age thinking (see Hay 1987; Zukav 1990).

This approach says that you ought to do what is in your interest. Altruism is seen either as hypocritical (it isn't really altruistic – people are always trying to make themselves look good or get to Heaven or whatever) or as actually corrosive of good ethics. So Rand, for example, argues that 'a selfless man cannot be ethical' (Rand 1997) because to act ethically from selfless motives means that you rely on some other authority outside yourself. Then, you are just doing what you are told, and there is little virtue in that.

Like Bentham's account of utility, it isn't just immediate, sensory, shallow interests that are important, but long-term, sustainable interests, and the things that will generally contribute to my overall happiness. And this is unlikely to be about being rich or having lots of sex. Smart people will realise this 'higher' interest and pursue that, and that can end up looking a lot like altruism, sociability, cooperation and other-directedness, as I argued in Chapter 4. In fact, the idea of the ethical professional we have been working with could be cast in ethical egoist terms.

According to ethical egoists, we are individuals first. We become social through *contract*. We see that things aren't working out too well, so, in our own interest, decide to make agreements with others about rules for living, etc. (Hobbes 1996, orig. 1651). While there is no absolute ground for morality, we build a moral code by contracting with each other to keep these rules, so that we can at least be secure. But even this doesn't really work, as Hobbes realises. Even if you and I make a contract to behave ourselves, it is still in my interest to break the contract if I can get away with it. Hobbes argues that the state is invented in order to enforce the contract, to supply punishment if the contract is broken.

Things to consider

Like lots of modern, liberal ideas, ethical egoism assumes that the individual is primary and prior to society and social forms. As Margaret Thatcher said, 'There is no such thing as society. There are individual men and women, and there are families' (Keay 1987). The theory seems blind to how commonplace and routine cooperation is, how people grow up to be social, how human beings routinely make decisions by asking other people about things, and so on. Does this view make sense?

Marxist ethics

Marx wouldn't have seen himself as writing a theory of ethics. However, as Rhodes notes (1986), there is a strong ethical dimension to Marx's work, and he deals with the world in a highly ethical way. What he claims to be doing is science, the establishment of laws of society. But at every turn, he wants to say that these social facts have deep implications for human behaviour and the state of human life – how things *ought* to be.

There are a number of components to Marx's ethical work. Briefly, these are:

- **A critique of morality**. Consistent with his general position that ideology is determined by the mode of production, Marx exposes conventional morality as a system of rules of behaviour that serve the interests of the ruling class. This includes marriage and sexual relations, property relations (including private ownership), notions of obedience and respect for authority. What he adds to standard consequentialist accounts is a pointed awareness of how morality serves particular interests (see above).
- **An idea of human nature**. Marx believed that human nature was dynamic and fluid, responding to the material conditions under which a people lived. However, there are some non-negotiables in his conception which have moral relevance. These include two core ideas. First, a notion of the human as deeply social, and therefore, once liberated from the distortions of class society, including the illusions of individualism and competition, as able to live peaceably and cooperatively with each other. And second, a notion of the human, and human nature, as being constructed through the interaction with Nature: in other words, through work. It is work that makes human beings what they are, whether meanspirited and low, or creative and joyful.

These ideas combine to place the kind of society that human beings live in, and especially the productive process of that society, under stern ethical judgement. If a mode of production establishes conditions of work that result in a degradation of human beings rather than their liberation into creative and joyful existence, that mode of production does not deserve to survive, and those who perpetuate its existence because it serves their particular interests are to be condemned.

Ethical action is therefore action that brings about a new and better system of social and economic relations. Marx is not squeamish about the means by which this should happen, and generally seems to indicate that any means necessary to bring about a more just society, including violent uprising, deception and expropriation, is legitimate. Unlike the utilitarians, it is not the balance of pains and pleasures that makes action legitimate, but about how a given action will contribute to the goal of demolishing this society and ushering in the new, classless and truly ethical community.

Marxist ethics does have a couple of problems. It suffers from what David Hume (1739/1985) identified as the *is-ought problem*, which can be summarised as 'is does not imply ought'. In other words, a fact does not imply that someone is obliged to do something about it. The fact that smoking might kill you doesn't by itself mean that morally, you shouldn't smoke. It might be a fact that workers receive less from productive processes than they contribute to them. It might be that some starve as a result. As a fact, this does not necessarily mean that anyone is obliged to do anything about that. That takes a moral view which Marx assumes but does not supply.

Deontological ethics

Where consequentialist approaches argue that ethical behaviour needs to be established from the consequences of an action, deontological ethical frameworks argue that morality is a quality of the act itself. Lying is not wrong because it tends to have bad results. It is wrong anyway, irrespective of whatever results, good or bad, that it has. According to deontological positions, if an action is wrong, the consequences cannot justify it.

Theories of *natural law*, including those which embrace inherent *human rights*, are included in the deontological category, as are theories which base ethics on an understanding of the will of God. Frameworks which are based on a *central ethical principle* fit here too, such as the fundamental obligation to keep contracts which underlies many *contractarian* positions. Immanuel Kant, probably the most famous philosopher of ethics outside the religious traditions, tends to be regarded as a deontologist. *Intuitionist* positions, which argue that people generally know what is right and wrong intuitively, are deontological too.

Typically, deontological ethics have:

- **Negative formulation.** Classically, deontological ethics tell you what you should not do ('Thou shalt not ...'), and it is OK to do the rest. Deontologists argue that this preserves the largest domain of personal freedom. Avoiding wrong actions leaves you a lot of things to do and to enjoy.
- **Limited scope.** Some things are wrong, some are right, and most things are neither right nor wrong but a matter of taste or prudence. There is nothing ethically wrong with having bad taste.
- **Personal responsibility.** In our earlier example about drinking coffee, the exploitation of peasants is something the exploiters are responsible for, not you. Your ethical decisions are restricted to your own actions.
- **A focus on motives and intentions.** The motive behind an action is what constitutes it as ethically right or wrong, not how the action turns out. It is not unethical to make a mistake (presuming that you have not been culpably negligent or ignorant in your action). And unintentionally doing good while in the process of pursuing evil does not mitigate the evil.
- **Objectivity.** Deontological ethics are better at avoiding the potential political bias of the ethical calculus, and the tendency of those in power to see their own pleasure and pain very well and to underestimate the feeling of the marginalised. For a deontologist, if an action is wrong, it is wrong no matter whether the king or the pauper does it.

Of course, deontological ethics has its own problems. First, what is the *basis* for believing that lying, or any other immoral act, belongs in the unethical basket? In other words, what is it about immoral acts that makes them immoral? Is it a revelation from God? Is it built into human beings somehow, either genetically or psychologically or spiritually?

Second, while a credible and rational ethics can be constructed on the basis of any of these beliefs, they only work if you share the beliefs. This may work very well at the level of a personal morality or in a single-ideology community, but it becomes less useful once the underlying belief is called into question. Of course, belief or non-belief does not make it so. Something might still be wrong even though lots of people don't see anything wrong with it. But, in the absence of shared belief, the only thing a deontologist can do is *assert* that something is wrong or right. In a pluralist world, and especially in the realm of social ethics, the absence of shared belief is the standard situation, not the exception.

In such an environment, deontological commentators (like the churches, for example) often resort to consequentialist justifications for their positions. But if consequentialism is OK as a last resort, why isn't it OK as a first resort?

Third, what happens in an ethical dilemma, when no matter what you do, there seems to be no way out of a situation without breaking one ethical principle or another? Is it possible in this case to do right? Or are both options wrong, but one less wrong than the other?

One of the slogans that has become commonplace in ethical discussion is that '*ought implies can*' (an idea that probably comes from Immanuel Kant's (1788/2005) *Critique of Practical Reason*). If you can't do something, no one can point the finger at you to say that, ethically, you should. In ethical dilemma, there is no action available which avoids breaking an ethical rule or duty. But this sets up a bit of a contradiction: if rightness is a quality of the act itself, how can it be right to pursue an action which is wrong in itself?

Deontologists have a number of ways of dealing with this problem. One of these is to establish a *hierarchy of values*. Thus, while certain actions are wrong in themselves, there are degrees of seriousness. Taking a life is usually high on the scale, telling lies rather lower. It is possible to establish a register of such values, either individually or as part of an ethical community (such as a youth work agency), which would then guide people in the event of an ethical dilemma. However, although there is often a broad consensus about what is wrong, the consensus disappears when people try to decide which transgression is more wrong than another. Natural law might tell us that lying and betrayal are wrong, but it does not tell us which is more wrong.

A second approach is to line up the alternatives with a *central ethical principle*. Examples of this are the 'law of love', common in Christian ethical frameworks. Which of the two alternatives is the more loving? Or Kant's *categorical imperative*, with its twin principles of respect for persons and the principle of universalisability. That is, you should only do something if you were OK for it to be a general rule, so that everyone did it. In youth work ethics, a principle such as 'empowerment' or 'the best interest of young people' might be employed to this end.

Frequently, deontologists resort either to consequentialism or to virtue ethics to resolve ethical dilemmas. Again, consequentialists argue that this is cheating. If consequentialist methods are OK to get you out of a sticky situation, why are they not OK in the first place?

Virtue-based ethics

Virtue-based ethics are not concerned so much with keeping the rules or of working out the line of action which will result in the greatest pleasure. Virtue-based ethics focus on the kind of person you want to become, the kind of community you want to live in, the kind of society you want to be a part of. As Democritus said, 'to live badly is not to live badly, but to spend a long time dying' (Freeman 1948). You become a good person by pursuing the virtues like courage, discipline, moderation and compassion, and you become a morally deficient person by slipping into vices like intemperance, laziness, cowardice or dishonesty. You might think of yourself as a good person, but giving yourself permission to lie will eventually turn you into a liar, not controlling your temper will make you violent and nasty, and pursuing indiscriminate sexual engagement (whether you are male or female) will make you a slut. When faced with a moral issue, the right question is 'What kind of person will this make me? What kind of person do I want to be?'

Virtue-based ethics also apply to organisations. An organisation can generate virtues in the people who work within it, the other organisations it interacts with, and in the members of the public it serves. And it can do the opposite, generating conflict and spite among its workers, aiming to destroy other organisations, misusing public money, and dealing with members of the public with disrespect and disregard.

The question, then, is obviously how you define goodness. Classically, a virtue-based ethics includes a list of values or virtues against which action can be measured (see Martin 1989), though there isn't necessarily any consensus about what should be on the list. In the helping professions, for example, objectivity or emotional disengagement is sometimes seen as a virtue, sometimes not (see Chapter 14).

Virtue-based approaches are common in professional ethics, where the ground is often too complex or variable to make deontological approaches useful. In such a circumstance, where too many situations emerge where the rules don't apply or simply don't work, it can be better to rely on the *integrity of the youth worker*, and to believe in and support their *struggle for goodness*, than to rely on codes or rules.

Things to consider

Kerry Young (2006) argues that the goal of youth work can be none other than the construction of a more virtuous society, and to challenge young people themselves to be more virtuous. What do you think of this claim?

Conclusion

This has been a very brief tour through the landscape of ethical theory. Massive amounts have been left out, and we have left out a lot of detail in what has been included. The work of Immanuel Kant especially, with his concern for the dignity of persons, has been influential in how ethics has been constituted in youth work and other human service professions. Hopefully, though, you have found one or other approach that resonates with you, and the discussion of consequentialist, deontological and virtue-based ethical approaches will have helped you put your own framework into a wider context, and helped give it some shape.

It might, however, just be confusing. There is a danger in this: a temptation to think that because there is no universal agreement on how to think ethically that ethics is arbitrary, a matter of whatever you want to believe is OK, or that you can't ever say what is right and wrong (Sommers 1985).

This is not an option. All of these thinkers would be very clear that some things are right and some are wrong, and would often agree about what they are. To be sure, there are dilemmas, where it is hard to work out which is the right thing to do, and there are sometimes disagreements, though these are often more on the surface than fundamental. But all that this means is that sometimes ethical thinking is hard work. It might be tempting to just withdraw into an easy relativism, in which whatever you think is OK, because it is all just too hard. In our field, that is a recipe for exploitation and damage. If work needs to be done, do the work.

There is a growing possibility also that there might be a synthesis between these different theoretical families. I can't see anything that requires us to use one and only one of these frameworks to inform our moral decision-making. It isn't as though the different theories come to wildly different conclusions, although the way they get there might be different. It may be that rule-thinking, consequence-thinking and character-thinking aren't that far apart. Maybe our rules, and our ideas about virtue, are the product of long experience of the consequences of people's actions. We might have a moral rule about cheating on your partner, for example, not to spoil people's fun, but because we have had thousands of years of experience of adultery. We know the risk of damage to relationships, and often to children, that adultery carries.

Individuals are often poor assessors of that risk, and just as often turn away from any such assessment if the action is something they want to do, or if they are frightened. We are also masters at self-deception. The moral rule holds people responsible for their actions if they choose to act in the face of existing moral guidance. It may be that swimming in a particular pool is safe under certain conditions, despite the fact that there are signs warning of crocodiles. Indeed, you might have swum there without harm before, and seen others do so. But if you take a group of young people there on a swimming expedition, and one gets eaten by a crocodile, you are absolutely and singularly responsible for that. The guidance was there, you chose to think you knew better, so you are responsible for that choice and any damage that ensues.

On the other side, consequentialism, in a changing world, can provide a check on the continuing relevance of a rule or how it is being applied. If the application of a rule is consistently producing widespread human suffering, it is a really good indication that the rule, or its application in this instance, is wrong.

And this brings us to the question of codes of ethics. Codes of ethics represent compilations of that collective wisdom, in the context of professional relationships and professional action. There is no agreement, by any means, that they are the best way to provide ethical guidance to youth workers. But at the moment, they don't have a lot of competitors, and as one of a range of tools for shaping ethical practice, they deserve a hearing.

7

CODES OF ETHICS

Summary

This chapter looks at codes of ethics in youth work, and their relationship with the development of youth work as a profession. It asks whether codes of ethics are able to help youth workers make ethical decisions, and whether they stimulate ethical debate or stifle it. Codes of ethics from the UK, North America, New Zealand and Australia are compared, and the common features across these codes are identified. Finally, the chapter discusses how codes of ethics are to be enforced, and whether and how penalties are to be applied for breaches of the code.

Codes of ethics, in our field at least, are a relatively recent phenomenon. That is probably true of the professions in general, with the outstanding exception of medicine: the Hippocratic Oath goes back to the fourth century BCE, and the first modern code of ethics for medicine to 1794 (BBC 2003). However, codes of ethics have been springing up among the professions (and other occupations too) since the 1930s, with the trend increasing over the last decade.

In youth work, interest in a code of ethics has been on the agenda from the late 1970s. In the UK, Brunel University's Regional Consultative Training Unit published a 1978 discussion paper on the subject (Banks 1999). A group of Australian youth workers drafted the Jasper Declaration (a statement on youth work social and political ethics) at the first National Youth Conference in 1977, and their concerns were developed enough to prompt a major national conference on a code of ethics in 1991 (Quixley and Doostkhah 2007). Martha Mattingly (1995) reports various initiatives in Canada and the USA from about 1985 onwards. New Zealand was later on the scene, with national discussions in 1995, codes of ethics being developed at the regional level from 1997, and a national draft in 2008 (National Youth Workers Network Aotearoa 2008). Youth workers in other countries, such as Malta, South Africa, Finland and Ireland, have been on a similar journey. However, the actual development of codes of ethics for youth work has been tentative and its adoption uneven.

Why a code of ethics?

The pressure to formalise codes of ethics has come from a number of different places. The massive worldwide surge of concern about the sexual exploitation of children has had a major impact, and youth work has certainly been among the professions implicated. The sexual exploitation of children is shocking, ethically unambiguous, and has compelled all of the professions who deal with children to look carefully at their ethics and their regulatory systems. More generally, codes of ethics present a partial solution for a society in which risk and the management of risk has become a major, perhaps the dominant, social process (Beck 1992). Other reasons include:

- professionalisation
- identity
- the relationship with the state
- drawing the line.

Professionalisation

Codes of ethics have always been linked to professionalisation. There is a logic to this. If Koehn (1994) is right about the ethical foundation of the professions, then a close association between the formal statement of ethics and the formal constitution of the profession is likely. In some cases, this has been the motive for developing a code. A consortium of associations of Child and Youth Care workers in North America generated a code specifically because it was part of the professional trait list identified by Greenwood in 1957, and so would form part of the claim to professional status (Greenwood 1957; Mattingly 2005).

Identity

A major driver in the formulation of codes of ethics has been the struggle to achieve clarity about what youth work is and what youth work does. Helena Barwick's review of youth work across Australia, New Zealand the UK (2006) identified lack of clarity as a major inhibition on the development of youth work practice and its wider recognition. She recommended two things to remedy this: training and a code of ethics. A code of ethics is as much as anything an identity statement: a collective and public declaration by a body of workers about the assumptions that form the basis of their work, and a public set of standards to which they can be held accountable.

The question of identity is important also to identify what is *not* youth work. The youth work 'brand' is worth something. It connotes a flexible, informal, respectful and potentially transformative engagement with young people, on their own terms. In television dramas and in the media generally, youth workers are cool, especially from the point of view of young people. It isn't surprising, then, that the brand gets appropriated, and a range of practitioners, from prison wardens in juvenile prisons to street evangelists, start to call themselves youth workers.

But then, how are young people to know what it is they are getting when someone introduces themselves as a youth worker? Traditions of youth work have been hard won and hard fought for. They need protecting.

More broadly, a code of ethics can be the kind of foundation document around which youth workers organise. Organising youth workers is difficult at the best of times (a colleague once likened it to herding cats), but a code of ethics can provide a kind of constitution for organising, not only for a professional association but around issue-based campaigns.

The relationship with the state

Governments have also had a project of disciplining the youth work sector, bringing it under closer control under the guise of 'accountability'. There has been an increasing sophistication in government techniques of control over the sector over the last 20 years, generally referred to as *managerialism*. Up until the mid-1970s, government funding was mainly in the form of grants to community organisations to support services proposed and initiated by the community. Often, services are now designed and initiated by governments and put out for tender on a payment-for-service basis. Agencies are now effectively agents of government, still with some scope for autonomous action, but within increasingly prescribed limits.

In this context, governments have been more and more directive about the way that youth workers do their job. Sharing information is becoming increasingly mandatory, with real complications for the pledge of confidentiality. Increasingly, workers are required to exercise punitive action against young people on behalf of governments. Youth workers have been involved in curfews and other street-clearing exercises, and processes which may be against the interests of young people, such as the punitive provisions in welfare to work programmes such as Australia's Work for the Dole programme. It is hard to see how the young person is your primary client when you have just cut off their income for missing an appointment.

Without a clear, collectively affirmed ethical position from which to argue, it is difficult for workers to refuse any line of action on the grounds that it is unethical. Workers or agencies making such a stand are left exposed as lone voices, vulnerable to retaliation or withdrawal of funding. The absence of a clear ethical position, in an environment in which resourcing is 'contestable', or where governments create a competitive market for the funding of services, can mean that funding will go to those agencies least inhibited by ethical constraints.

In this environment, youth work doesn't have a choice about being disciplined: it's just a question of who does it and on what terms. A code of ethics means that we decide what standard we will hold ourselves to. Like medical practitioners, who were able collectively to refuse to supervise the death penalty in the USA by invoking professional standards (Lichtenberg 1996), a code of ethics can provide a foundation for resistance to various government interventions which may be oppressive to young people or in violation of their civil rights.

Drawing the line

The core purpose of a code of ethics, however, is to discipline practice in the interests of protecting the relationship that we have with young people and protecting young people within that relationship. We might think that we are clear about what ethical practice is – about what you should do and what you should not do. However, this awareness is apparently not universal. Not only is the sexual exploitation of young people by youth workers not rare, there are a range of other practices or incidents which experienced workers will point to, including:

- selling drugs to young people (or buying them from them)
- sharing pornographic videos
- buying electronic goods from young people
- embezzling agency funds
- using agency vehicles extensively for private business
- 'permanent loans' of electronic, sporting or camping equipment to workers
- using agency funds for home renovations
- turning up for work drunk or stoned
- giving police access to young people's files.

Are the youth workers involved in these practices evil people? Generally not. Sometimes, they were people who got into desperate straits through addictions of various kinds (especially gambling) or relationship breakdown. Sometimes, they just weren't thinking clearly enough, and weren't talking to their colleagues, or their colleagues either didn't know what they were up to or weren't thinking clearly enough either.

More often, a practice emerges gradually, and often collectively: it might become the practice in an agency for workers to borrow equipment, to take it home, without a strict reckoning. We tell each other it's OK. Then people forget they have it, or they tell themselves it never gets used in the agency, and it gets good use at home, or they work a lot at home, using this equipment. And the boundary between work and non-work isn't that clear anyway. And then they have a whole lot of equipment at home that, as far as any objective observer is concerned, they have stolen.

A code of ethics draws a line in the sand or, more often, insists that a line must be drawn (wherever you decide the line is). If there is a line, you might know when you have crossed it. We are just as adept at moving the line to suit ourselves, but if we are in dialogue with our colleagues about this, there is some mutual accountability in the process, and it makes us think, slows us down a bit at least. Often, we become adept at arguing to ourselves that while an action would generally not be right, in this instance, it seems justified. An external standard gives us a kind of checklist against which to measure our actions, or a way to hear the cracking when we start to walk on thin ice.

A code of ethics can also provide a core for other more specific guidance documents, such as agency policy manuals or codes of behaviour. In the next chapter, we'll look at how that might work in a bit more detail.

> ## Summary: a code of ethics can be used
>
> 1. To protect the youth work relationship, and young people in the relationship.
> 2. To name unethical or suspect practice.
> 3. To guide us in new or difficult situations.
> 4. To keep ourselves (and each other) accountable.
> 5. To provide the basis for organisation.
> 6. To provide a core for more detailed policy development at the agency level.
> 7. To improve the status of the profession in the public sphere.
> 8. To clarify our identity as youth workers, and to identify non-youth workers.
> 9. To defend ourselves against being co-opted into oppressive practices.

The limits of codes of ethics

A code of ethics generally won't tell you what to do, not most of the time anyway. No code imaginable would be able to cover the range of contexts, cultural groups and issues that youth workers cover even in a single day's work, and neither should it. A code needs to encourage youth workers to think ethically through whatever situations they face, and to talk together about them, and to give them the tools to do that. It might offer some starting points, and the principles that might be important in coming to a decision, but a code mostly won't tell you the answer. So a code is no substitute for intelligent, collegial, reflective practice.

Example

A multi-service youth work agency in Perth, Western Australia, has the Code of Ethics printed on credit-card sized laminated cards which are carried by workers. When decisions are being made that have ethical implications, the team decides which of the clauses in the Code are relevant. Each team member will then be allocated to a single clause, and will put the case as though theirs is the only clause to be considered. Informed by this accumulated argument, a collective decision is made.

Codes are open to interpretation (Quixley and Doostkhah 2007). Generally, they have been written that way. As open documents within which people from diverse ideological persuasions can nevertheless find meaning and some core agreement about what working ethically might mean in a situation. If they aren't open documents, not only do they only appeal to whatever minority shares the ideology of the writers, but they also become obsolete quickly, as professional cultures and ideologies change. This openness does mean that there is room for perverse interpretation, twisting the meaning of things until they bear no relation to what was intended in the document, or justifying behaviour on the basis of such a perverse interpretation.

Again, a code is an aid to ethical thinking, not a substitute for it. If a practice appears suspect but can be made to comply with the letter of a code of ethics, then either the code is written badly or the interpretation is disingenuous. Being able to justify behaviour by reference to a code doesn't necessarily make the behaviour right. This isn't taxation law we're talking about, where you can go free on a technicality.

Four codes: a comparison between codes in the UK, Australia, North America and New Zealand

The four major codes covered here (British, Australian, New Zealand and North American) emerged through different processes and with different motivations across these four constituencies. The UK (England and Wales) code (National Youth Agency 2002) was drafted by committee, with the expert guidance of social work ethicist Sarah Banks. The North American code (Mattingly 1995), under the guidance of academic Martha Mattingly and others, gathered existing documents both within child and youth care circles and in cognate professions such as social work and nursing, and by a combination of committee and individual labour, forged a composite document. In the Australian case (Youth Affairs Council of Western Australia 2003), I wrote the initial drafts, which were refined through a series of workshops and seminars with practitioners. The New Zealand code began with the Canterbury Youth Workers Collective, which started with the Australian code and reshaped it for the New Zealand (and particularly Maori) situation. It was then taken up and redrafted by the National Youth Workers' Network of Aotearoa (NYWNA), which is currently consulting and promoting the code for authoritative adoption (National Youth Workers Network Aotearoa 2008).

These different histories and processes, and the different youth work cultures in each country, have shaped the documents that now exist and the status they hold. The most authoritative is the North American code, which is the undisputed standard for child and youth care professionals in the USA and Canada. Child and Youth Care professionals there are well advanced in a range of disciplinary mechanisms, involving regulation and deregulation. However, this currently has no recognition in law.

The Australian code currently has voluntary status (i.e. workers or agencies sign up voluntarily, either formally or informally, under the umbrella generally of the Youth Affairs Councils in each jurisdiction) in Western Australia, the Australian Capital Territory and New South Wales, with an adapted version adopted in Victoria. It is seen as authoritative and compelling in those jurisdictions, if not mandatory. Its status is strongest in Western Australia, where signing up to the code is a condition of membership of the Youth Affairs Council and the Western Australian Association of Youth Workers. Currently, no enforcement or regulatory processes exist.

The UK code generally is seen as a document for guidance and discussion. It does not claim authoritative status, and no regulatory mechanism is currently being discussed. The originating body, the National Youth Agency (NYA), does not have jurisdiction in Scotland and Northern Ireland. There is no code of ethics in either of those two nations, although value statements expressed through official guidance documents promoted by such organisations as the Standards Council in Scotland do some of the same work, and a code of ethics is on the agenda for sector development in Northern Ireland (Transport and General Workers' Union 2008). Workers are registered in the UK by virtue of their training, and the training is regulated by a standards framework which includes a values framework.

The New Zealand code is of more recent origin, but is being energetically pursued by the NYWNA with the strong support of government. A code of ethics is seen there as a core strategy for establishing quality, clarity and accountability in the sector, and is likely to see official national endorsement in the near future.

The codes look a bit different on the surface. Size, apparently, does not matter. The Australian code was designed to fit on a single sheet of paper. The New Zealand code is 17 pages long, with the North American and British codes falling somewhere in between. The Australian code is designed to be supported by a number of supplementary documents, including a commentary further explaining each of the clauses and a series of worked examples. It also expects that the detail of how each clause will work out in practice will be developed at the level of individual agencies or perhaps sector groupings, such as residential workers or detached youth workers. The New Zealand code includes more explanatory material within the text of the code, and has more detail regarding explicit rules. The British code tends to stay with broad principles rather than particular duties or expectations. The North American code is set out as a range of responsibilities that the youth worker has to themselves, the client, the employing agency, the profession and society.

The tone of each is also different. The British code reflects its stance as a discussion document. It is explanatory, engaging in tone. At the other end of the scale, the Australian code is direct, assertive, declamatory. The North American code takes the form of a set of competences or standards to be met.

Youth work practice in each setting is grounded in a particular conceptual framework. The Australian and New Zealand codes are based in discourses of advocacy, with overt connections in the New Zealand code to concepts of human rights, and implicit connections in the Australian one. The British document is based in discourses of education, especially the informal education tradition, and with strong connections to concepts of social justice and equality. The North American code is grounded in developmental psychology, especially where it connects with social psychology. The influence of the human ecology tradition, especially Ulrich Bronfenbrenner (who was interested in the development of children and young people within their social context (Bronfenbrenner 1979)) is clear in the conceptual work.

However, despite these differences of language and discourse, none of these codes disagrees. Different elements might be emphasised in one or the other, and some might have clauses that are absent in others, but there is clearly a commonality here, a tradition that is recognisably youth work regardless of the different histories and influences in each country, and some core affirmations that reach across their respective geographies. All of the codes highlight:

- That the young person/young people are at the centre of the work, and that youth workers' first duty is to them.
- The exclusion of young people, and the need to redress this through the opportunity to make their voices heard, and to participate and be included fully in political and economic processes.
- That youth work practice should avoid discriminating against marginalised groups of young people, and to actively redress such discrimination where it occurs.
- That youth workers are obliged to make sure that they are skilled, competent and knowledgeable, to keep up to date and keep developing, and to recognise when they have reached their limits and others need to be brought on board.
- The need to collaborate with other professionals.
- That youth workers need to be scrupulous about confidentiality.
- The need to be careful about the boundary between the professional relationship and other kinds of relationship with the young person, especially sexual relationships. All but the NYA code ban sexual engagement outright.
- That young people are able and competent to make choices for themselves, and that youth workers should be facilitating and developing their capacity and opportunity to do that.
- That young people exist in a social environment, and that the work extends also to the social environment.
- That the work includes a political element.
- That youth workers need to be aware of their own values, and reflective around those values in their work.
- That youth work environments need to be safe for young people.

This commonality is, I think, powerful. Despite very different histories and structural arrangements, youth workers across the world have come to the same conclusions about how the profession is to be constituted ethically. An international code of ethics, difficulties in wording aside, would be very possible on the basis of these documents. Youth work tends to see itself as a local, geographically specific practice. The documents reveal an international consensus about a youth work identity, and what is important in constituting youth work practice, despite local or national variation or specificity.

Enforcement... and effectiveness

A great deal of debate around codes of ethics has gone into how to discipline youth workers who transgress. The standard mechanism in the established professions is that the professional body has a disciplinary process, usually a board or committee of some kind, that receives complaints from clients and judges their legitimacy. If a complaint is upheld, a practitioner can have a range of sanctions applied, including temporary or permanent deregistration and withdrawal of their licence to practise.

In most countries, however, there is no professional youth workers' association, let alone disciplinary committees; no professional registration or licence to practise; and no legal backing for sanctions. At this point in time, there are no binding structures to ensure compliance with whatever codes of ethics might be in place.

Some commentators, such as Judith Bessant, have suggested that a code of ethics has

> serious limitations unless accompanied by specific mechanisms to give it material effect. To be successful, codes need to be regulatory and enforceable by an organization that adjudicates complaints of breaches of the code. Without the backing of legislative mandating, and proper sanctions (including the power to strike off practitioners for misconduct), the effectiveness of a code of conduct can only be minimal.

> (Bessant 2004: 28)

The claim is also used by Quixley and Doostkhah (2007) to argue that codes of ethics necessarily involve formal professionalisation, necessarily invoke disciplinary procedures like registration and deregistration, necessarily enshrine a minority as gatekeepers of the profession, and necessarily constitute a reduction in youth workers' autonomy and the profession becoming more conservative.

This might be true: it would be interesting to find out. These are factual claims, not philosophical ones. Research could determine the effect of codes of ethics in situations where these sanctions have been absent, and compare them with situations where they have been in place. Informal sanctions might in fact be much more powerful than official sanctions. You might be able to convince your conscience that some questionable practice is OK, but an awareness of how your colleagues will see your action if it ever got out (and someone always knows!) is a strong deterrent.

Another mechanism is the internal disciplinary processes of employing organisations. Employers do have access to disciplinary procedures, with legal backing and financial consequences, so workers can be sacked. Codes of ethics can be powerful in giving agencies clarity about what behaviour is acceptable in programmes for which they have responsibility.

The evidence to this point seems to be that where a code of ethics is active, workers are more aware of the need to factor ethics into their decision-making, to argue with each other about ethics, and to challenge each other. They are clearer about what youth work is and what it isn't, and struggle with employer or funding body demands that threaten to compromise their ethical position. They are more strident about the prerogatives of young people, not less. On the ground, a strong, well-promoted, active code of ethics has not stifled ethical conversation as some critics (e.g. Dawson 1994; Quixley and Doostkhah 2007) thought that it would.

Conclusion

A code of ethics is not a guarantee of ethical practice, nor is it risk free. If the existence of a code of ethics makes workers smug, thinking that the ethical questions of practice are all sorted out and that they can just follow policy and obey orders and do what they have always done, then that is dangerous. If a code is drafted but then left to sit idle and passive, or if workers aren't aware that it exists, you might be better off without one.

A code of ethics is a live document, constantly reviewed, and able to shift with shifts in discourse and understanding but also to resist the winds of mere fashion and the pressure of outside influence. It can be a compass for a profession which is dependent on the powerful for the resources it needs to do its job, a statement of identity for a profession that has earned the right to be what it is, a defence against encroachment from those who would use its reputation to further their own interests, a check for practice in which workers have high degrees of independence and autonomy. If practitioners are trained in the kind of ethical thinking that makes the code live in their hands, if they are able to engage critically with their document, if they feel like it belongs to them, a code of ethics can be the backbone of authentic, principled youth work practice.

Part Three

Ethical Issues and Conflicts

8

ETHICS AND AGENCY POLICY

Summary

This chapter is about how to work with ethics, including using a code of ethics, to maintain a line of practice in organisations that enhances and deepens our youth work. For example, we will discuss how to write agency policy in ways that connect to an agency's ethical commitments. The environment isn't always sympathetic to youth work practice, however. The chapter discusses how to work strategically with existing policy that is difficult or wrong, including, at the limit, the obligations and risks of 'whistleblowing', when employees or other insiders find themselves in the position of having to publicly call their organisations to account.

It isn't just individuals who make decisions, who act, and who therefore are ethical subjects, responsible for the ethics of their decisions. Organisations do too. This has been conceptualised for a long time in Western legal and philosophical thinking as the notion of the 'corporate person'. This is why groups of people become 'incorporated', to give this 'corporate person' legal status so that the law can treat them in the same way they do a 'natural person' – they are able to own property, to sign contracts, to make decisions and be legally responsible for those decisions.

Organisational processes and procedures have become more detailed and formalised over the last couple of decades, as the detail of external legal obligations has increased and as organisations have got bigger. It is typical now for local government or not-for-profit organisations to have detailed written internal codes or policies which lay out standard operational procedures, rules for behaviour, lines of management and decision-making, levels of authority... and ethical expectations.

Agency policy presents a range of opportunities, and challenges, for ethical youth work. If the organisation's culture is sympathetic to youth work and youth work's way of working, agency policy can relieve you from the burden of ethical decision-making in routine circumstances. If an ethical problem crops up regularly, an organisation can make a decision which is then written down and can be used in all equivalent situations. In this way, you can increase efficiency and fairness while building an ethical culture or tradition for the organisation which enriches the agency and its workers.

This is especially so if the agency has a high turnover of staff, or a large number of untrained staff or volunteers. The policy framework guides action in most situations, meaning that the organisation is less dependent on a worker's training or capacity for sophisticated professional judgement. Where a situation is difficult, it can be referred upwards to more senior workers for decision. So a policy framework can maximise the delegation of work because the work is always guided by the policy framework. It can enable workers to have more freedom and responsibility than they would otherwise have had.

But such an environment may not be sympathetic to youth work practice. A lot of youth work happens under the sponsorship of organisations which are not specifically youth work-focused, and workers may find themselves having to fight against agency policy or the requirement to act in ways that go against their idea of what youth work is. Over time, the preference that many managers and administrators have for neatness can mean that the informality, spontaneity and egalitarian style of youth work becomes increasingly constrained and rule-bound, and that the interests of young people fade in favour of the prerogatives of the agency. However things begin, the agency culture can end up being hostile to young people and to youth work practice.

Ethics and framing agency policy: Codes of Ethics, Codes of Practice, Codes of Behaviour

First, some things about policy.

1. Policy is not handed down from God. It is a result of human decision-making. It can always be changed.
2. Policy is a way of avoiding the work of making decisions by creating a standard decision for a particular situation. Whose responsibility is it to lock up? The last person to leave the building. Where do the car keys go? In the box. Where policy seems unjust, unfair or unworkable, the first point of analysis is to work out what decision is being avoided.
3. Policy is never free of politics. Standard decisions are always made in someone's interest. It takes persistence and courage to keep the interests of young people at the top of the list.
4. Policy is designed for standard cases. No matter how detailed or clever the policy, there will always be a situation where the standard approach will result either in a stupid decision or in an injustice being done. All policies need the flexibility to be waived in particular circumstances, and there will always be someone who has the power to authorise a non-standard solution.
5. Writing good policy isn't easy. Most policy documents will need constant attention, constant revision, to make them work.

Having said that, Amanda Sinclair (1996) has set out a model for ways to integrate ethics into policy formation at the agency level. Like lots of similar frameworks, she tries to clarify what is happening by separating out the 'deeper principle' questions from the 'pragmatic day-to-day' ones. One way to do this is for policy manuals and similar documents to separate out *codes of ethics*, *codes of practice*, and *codes of behaviour* (simplifying her model a little). Ideally, the three levels of thinking ought to be consistent with each other.

Codes of ethics were discussed in the last chapter. At the agency level, the code of ethics could be the standard professional code for youth work in your jurisdiction, or it could be specific to the agency, or it could be the standard professional code adapted and supplemented for the situation of your agency. The clauses of a code of ethics will usually be pretty general.

Codes of practice refer to the way that ethical clauses play out in particular contexts – still at the level of principle, but firmly applied to a particular situation. Banks (2003) calls these 'practice principles' as opposed to 'ethical principles'. Breaking a 'practice principle' might not be unethical *as such*, though it might be in a particular situation, because of the way it relates to and supports a deeper ethical principle. It isn't unethical, for example, to talk to a journalist. But if an organisation regulates which employees can talk to the media in order to protect clients, it probably would be. 'Don't talk to the media unless you have been authorised to do so' would be a practice principle.

Codes of behaviour refer to actual acts: what you actually *do*. 'Return the car keys to the box, and sign off the booking sheet.' 'Talk to the young person about the agency's position on confidentiality, explaining (a), (b), (c) and (d).' 'Send out parental permission slips at least a fortnight beforehand.'

Here are a couple of examples from a policy manual we developed for a youth centre in Western Australia (Sercombe 2004). The code of ethics clauses are taken from the Australian *Code of Ethics for Youth Work* (Youth Affairs Council of Western Australia 2003).

Record keeping

Code of ethics

Self-care

Ethical youth work practice is consistent with preserving the health of youth workers.

Confidentiality

Information provided by young people will not be used against them, nor will it be shared with others who may use it against them. Young people should be made aware of the contextual limits to confidentiality, and their permission sought for disclosure. Until this happens, the presumption of confidentiality must apply.

(Continued)

(Continued)

Self-awareness

Youth workers are conscious of their own values and interests, and approach difference in those with whom they work with respect.

Code of practice

Records should:

- Be stored securely, with access only by authorised persons.
- Be consistent with limits to confidentiality negotiated with the young person.
- Not implicate young people in illegal activity should records be required by police or other authorities.
- Be consistent with the provisions of the Privacy Act, understanding that young people may ask to see their file.
- Be legible and well-organised.
- Be truthful.

Code of behaviour

You are required to keep the following records.

1. **Reflective Journal**. Each day, you should write a bit about your day, who you met, what happened, what you learnt, what questions you had or what you didn't understand. Noting the young people you had contact with will help you remember names and will also help you make the most out of your clinical supervision. The reflective journal may be kept personal and confidential if you wish, though you can be required to produce it by a court of law.
2. **Weeksheet**. This notes the broad areas of activity each day, including the amount of time that you spent in different kinds of activity. It helps with time management because it makes you keep track of how much time you are spending where. It also helps your supervisor intervene if you are working too hard.
3. **Data collection form**. This form should be filled out at the end of every shift. The data is required by our funding bodies and will be the basis of our claim that we have met our obligations and that the service is effective.
4. **Case management notes**. Where a young person is being case managed by the Service or is in formal counselling, a client file is opened in accordance with agency policy and detailed notes of every counselling or case management session are kept.

However, a particular subject within a policy manual may not need all three levels of commentary. The behaviour may flow obviously from the code of ethics, or you might not need to specify behaviours once the code of practice is made clear. So, for example:

Drug use

The agency aims to help young people control their use of drugs, to eliminate high-risk drug use, and minimise the harm of their drug use. As such, it is important that our own drug use is consistent with these aims.

Code of ethics

Duty of care

The youth worker avoids exposing young people to the likelihood of further harm or injury.

Code of practice

1. We will not purchase, use or supply any restricted psychotropic drug in the company of young people. This includes alcohol and tobacco as well as the illegal drugs. Caffeine is unrestricted.
2. We will not appear in public in an intoxicated state whether on duty or not.
3. We will not turn up for work in any way impaired by any restricted psychotropic drug.

It takes a bit of practice to get a feel for what belongs in a code of ethics, code of practice and code of behaviour. Once you get it, though, it can work quite well.

But what about ethical conflict with your employing organisation?

Ethical conflict can arise from a number of sources. You may have a different ideological position from your employer, so you might interpret principles differently. As a feminist or a socialist, you might struggle working for an organisation that has a focus on business enterprise training as a path to individual advancement. As an atheist, you might struggle working for a faith-based organisation that sees religious conversion as important.

Part of this is obviously about your own choices: what jobs you apply for, and with what organisations. However, most situations will require some accommodation of values and ethics. This does not mean, ever, that you 'leave your values at the door'. It does mean working collaboratively: maintaining an ongoing dialogue to find common ground, and working together on the basis of that common ground wherever we can. And being humble enough to live with the fact that not everything is perfect. You won't be able to do some things because your organisation or your colleagues won't support that. Usually, though, there is enough common ground to create space for plenty to be done.

More commonly, your employer may not be youth work-driven, in which case, while the young person is your primary client, they may not be for your organisation. The job might have been advertised as a youth work job, but the organisation may not really understand what youth work is, and may not create the space for youth work to be done. This can, and does, lead to conflict where the interests of young people and other stakeholders collide.

There is no easy answer to this one. However, advocating for the rights of young people in an environment that doesn't particularly acknowledge that they do have rights isn't unusual for youth workers. It is the situation we face all the time in the media, in public forums, in collaborative partnerships, and with funding bodies. Most of the time, we have to roll with the punches, see if we can find another way, find space in the gaps to do what young people need us to do. At the limit, it may be that you decide you need to resign rather than act against the interests of young people – depending on how significant the issue is. If you do, of course, you need to consider the place that you leave young people in.

Things to consider

Ethically, resignation always needs to be an option. It is dangerous to be in a position where you just can't afford to resign. At some level, organisations seem to know when that is the case, when they have got you, when you can't afford to say no. And that is precisely the situation when the interests of young people start to be compromised.

Beyond that, however, it is down to your skills of negotiation and social change. A decent conversation about strategies for change would take rather more room than we have here, but it is important to work out what your organisation really needs out of the situation, and then to try to meet that need without compromising the core interests of young people.

Whistleblowing

Sometimes an organisation is acting unethically no matter how you cut it. Money allocated for services for young people may be being spent on someone's unrelated pet project, or to buy property, or on services for their own children or members of their church, to the exclusion of young people who really need it. The agency may be deliberately falsifying service data, or they may be using the media to promote the organisation, with obvious harm to clients.

In such a case, I think there is an ethical obligation to act. The standard process would be to raise the problem with your supervisor and leave it with him or her to follow up (though the problem may be with your supervisor!). It might be a good idea to talk about it in confidence with someone you trust first, just to check your assessment of the situation. If you can see that no action has been taken, there may be an ethical obligation to take it further, perhaps to management above the level where the problem is happening, maybe to someone on the board of governors or its equivalent. Hopefully, the organisation will see the wrong and fix it.

While it should never be the first step (or even the second or third), it might *ultimately* be necessary to go public with the issue: to the parent organisation, the funding body, the media, or the police. An employee or insider who exposes unethical behaviour in an organisation is often referred to as a *whistleblower*.

If you find yourself in that position, don't expect the organisation to thank you. Long experience with whistleblowers tells us that organisations don't nec-essarily react kindly to their ethical deficiencies being pointed out, especially by junior staff. And that in the conflict, whistleblowers usually lose. So building your defences and alliances is important prior to taking the issue on, especially prior to going public. Before you step out, do the research.

Preparing for the journey

1. Read up on whistleblowing. It may be a difficult journey, and it is important not to be naïve. Count the cost before you set out.
2. Find out what protection there is for whistleblowing in your jurisdiction, and in your organisation, at least on paper. See if there are any precedents.
3. Contact organisations that are set up to support and protect whistleblowers. There is a lot of information on the internet.
4. Talk to your family about what you intend to do, and make sure you have their support.
5. Ditto for colleagues, inside and outside the organisation, that you trust. Choose carefully, and it might be an idea to formally contract loyalty and confidentiality.
6. Contact the union. And if you aren't a member, join.
7. Make sure you have your facts straight. Rumour is not enough.
8. Document everything: names, times, dates, places, content. Keep a backup copy in a safe place.
9. It may be impossible to continue working in this organisation. You should think about an exit strategy if that is the case.

Courage, in ethical terms, is one of the classic virtues. Taking on unethical behaviour in your organisation (or, indeed, anywhere) can take a lot of it.

Conclusion

Working well with your organisation is a necessary part of ethical practice. You have ethical obligations to your employer by virtue of the contract that you have with them and the undertakings you have made as a part of that contract, and the position of trust they give you as a result. However, these obligations do not over-ride the prior ethical obligation you have to young people. The organisation is a vehicle for you to meet your obligations to young people, not the other way round.

Any organisation is a mechanism for aggregating and mobilising power (see Chapter 15). You can't get much done as an individual. The mobilisation of power is critical if we are to achieve anything with and for young people: it is a good and necessary and productive thing. But power corrupts, and any organisation is prone also to corruption (see Chapter 17). This is part of the reason why reflective practice, mutual accountability, and checks and balances within organisations are so important.

It is also why a professional's obligation is always also to retain some independence of thought and action. We can never become 'company men' or 'company women' because our loyalty and commitment to the organisation will always be secondary to our commitment to young people. If an organisation hires youth workers (or indeed any professional), they need to do so on that basis.

9

GOVERNMENT MONEY

Summary

This chapter explores the ethical tensions that exist in the relationship between youth work and governments, especially around the terms of financial support. While youth work and governments have always needed each other, their common interest is partial. Young people are the primary client of youth workers, but they are rarely so for governments, who have their own and other powerful interests to satisfy. The pursuit of integrity in the relationship needs careful ethical assessment to avoid youth workers becoming a mere servant of governments in the containment and control of young people on one hand, and devious and deceptive in their soliciting for financial support on the other.

Youth work has never been in a position of being financially independent. For all of its history, youth work has depended on governments, churches or the philanthropy of those with means to support its work (Jeffs and Smith 1999a). This support has rarely been either fulsome or reliable. With rare exceptions, youth work has been accustomed to working with bare-bones, short-term budgets, and to be constantly in danger of collapse due to lack of money.

The reasons for this are clear enough. Youth work serves a constituency which is itself marginalised economically. Medicine, law and the clergy have at least some clients who are well-to-do and prepared to pay (sometimes generously) for the service they receive. Other professions, such as social work, teaching and nursing, have been able to find a place on the inside of the state and its institutions, and a reasonably clear role in meeting its interests, so have attracted more reliable government sponsorship. Youth work has always been ambivalent in its relationship to the state and less reliable in furthering the state's interests.

Youth work and the state

I argued in Chapter 3 that the existence of youth work was due to the exclusion of young people from the common wealth and the constant risk that exclusion would slide into disengagement, with subsequent costs for the young person and the society around them. Youth workers engage young people, with the side-effect of some reduction in social costs, while governments fund youth work to reduce social costs, acknowledging that engagement may be the only way to do it.

The common interest of youth work and the state is, however, very partial. It shouldn't be, but it is. Notwithstanding the rhetoric, most governments are not really interested in the empowerment of young people. If they were, they would give them the vote. Mostly, governments see young people as a risk factor that needs to be managed: they want young people contained. If youth work could guarantee an orderly, predictable progression of young people through adolescence to orderly and predictable adulthood, that would be another matter – and we would see youth work budgets improve dramatically. But that is almost exactly the opposite of the way that youth workers work. And if young people are our primary client, and governments are busy maintaining systems dedicated to the exclusion and disempowerment of young people, that places us a priori in some degree of tension.

Theoretically, governments in a liberal democracy are elected to serve the interests of the constituency. A more realistic assessment is that regardless of the pretext or platform a political party came to power on, or whatever constituencies they represent, their first priority is to win and retain power. Put another way, the primary client of government is generally government. While there may be principled exceptions to this, governments will (almost) always serve their own interests first.

If governments' own interest is their first priority, their second priority is the interests of business. The state in a capitalist society, Marx argued, is a capitalist state (Lenin 1919/1972), and on this, he was right. Whatever a political party's philosophy might say (whether socialist or environmentalist or whatever), on achieving power, the interests of business become paramount. There isn't anything sinister about this, and it doesn't presume conspiracy. The survival of governments is dependent on the health of the economy, and the health of the economy, in a capitalist society, depends on business being happy. In addition, in most Western societies, re-election depends on the capacity to attract staggering amounts of money in election campaign contributions, and that kind of money only exists within the business community. Governments (of whatever stripe) alienate business at their peril.

This is the *realpolitik* within which we live and work. Occasionally, individual politicians and (slightly more occasionally) political parties may have a real commitment to young people, and to youth work as a means for improving conditions for young people. A little less rarely, a *rhetoric* of commitment to young people and/or youth work might be around, like the 'Priority One' campaign by the Hawke Labor Government in Australia in the late 1980s, or the Scottish Nationalist Party's policy to lower the voting age to 16. But unemployment rates in excess of 25% continued for young people in Australia through the 1990s, and the lowering of the voting age in Scotland remains unenacted at the point of writing. Rhetoric isn't always followed by real and sustained commitment, or by significant investment. This isn't a cynical view: just a realistic assessment of the political realities.

Dealing with the state and finding space for youth work

This environment has obvious ethical consequences. When youth workers are applying for funding, they need to pitch their proposals in terms that are attractive to governments, who are primarily interested (perhaps benevolently, to varying degrees) in the containment and control of young people. In order to attract the resources they need to do their work, youth workers have to meet that interest, while creating enough space for empowering, liberating, developmental youth work with young people. Ethically, this needs to happen without signing up to the repression of young people (becoming what Poynting and White (2004) call 'soft cops') on the one hand, or actually lying on the other (Jeffs and Smith 1999a).

So how do youth workers work with integrity, given these conflicts of interest?

One approach is to say whatever you need to say to get the contract, then do what you want to do once you have the money. On the face of it, this is an exercise in bad faith at least, and in lying at worst. An ethical justification would require the relationship with government and the ensuing contract to be excluded from the ethical consideration. The argument might run like this:

- Government is oppressive with respect to young people.
- Government is therefore an enemy.
- Government has therefore lost the right to be dealt with as legitimate and as a partner. The 'game' is different, and the exploitation of government, including chicanery, avoidance of obligation and cheating is justified.

There are a number of problems with this approach, and any approach in which certain human relationships are excluded from the ethical circle. Fundamentally, once any person (including a corporate person like a government department) is declared to be outside ethical obligation, anything is justified.

A more immediate and pragmatic problem, however, is that government accountability measures have become more sophisticated in recent years, and if you really have no intention of meeting the prescribed outcomes, or lie about your performance indicators, there is a good chance of being discovered. That could have serious consequences for your agency and its projects with young people. The likelihood (and, indeed, the living reality) is that it would also have consequences for the sector, leading to intensified accountability and policing measures, diverting time and resources from actual work with young people.

While the question of truth-telling isn't black and white (see Bok 1978 for the detail), and a reluctance to tell the truth, the whole truth, and nothing but the truth is sometimes justified, it is generally unethical to make statements which we know to be contrary to the facts. And from a virtue-based ethics point of view, the problem is that once you become accustomed to lying, you are a liar.

Making space for youth work

A more adequate answer is about the degree of closure in the instruments (the proposals, contracts or agreements) through which partnerships between funding bodies and youth workers are constructed. If the relationship is in the form of a funding agreement, for example, the agreement can only be set out in the most general terms. No contract can specify the day-to-day workings of a project, or the details of the way that youth workers will relate to young people, or what they will and won't talk about.

> Lots of youth work happens in the *spaces between* the 'outcomes' and 'deliverables' prescribed by funding bodies. The skill of youth workers lies in finding and working those spaces, while keeping the requirements of the funding contract.

In a contractual agreement, there is no obligation of full disclosure (unless, of course, that is part of the agreement). We are under no obligation to disclose the philosophies and principles from which we are working, all the objectives of every project, the detail of every activity we engage with, the content of every conversation, or what our other sources of funding might be. Within the tightest of funding contracts, there is space to do what we do. Of course, it is a matter of judgement as to whether the amount of space available to do youth work within a given project or setting is worth our (and the young person's) while.

This is one way in which the relationship with a funding body is different from the relationship with a young person. The relationship with a funding body is a *contract*, an exchange, and a commitment to complete a task. The relationship with a young person is a *covenant*, in which there is a commitment to the person, not just to the task. There is an obligation to be open and truthful with young people we work with, including letting them know the objectives of the project they are participating in, the sources of funding if they are interested, and the motivations of the funders. Openness with contract partners is on a need to know basis.

Second, youth work has a lot more power in the relationship than it often realises. Governments generally don't know how to engage young people. The standard mechanisms have typically already failed. Funding programmes need to give youth workers enough autonomy to be able to do their job: if they don't, it doesn't work, and young people still aren't engaged. Governments from time to time try to tighten their funding provisions, requiring more structured activities, greater accountability for curriculum and content, more detailed reporting of attendance and participation. But as they do, young people start dropping out and the project loses effectiveness.

Youth workers have often been able to win a bigger space for youth work to happen in negotiations with funding bodies because they clearly know what to do: they are clear and confident about what needs to happen for this group of young people to be engaged, or this issue to be dealt with. Often, governments just don't have the intelligence (both in the regular meaning and in the sense of information!) to be able to offer alternatives to the proposals that youth workers put forward, or, often enough, even to understand their full implications.

Third, language is never that precise; it is always open to interpretation. What a funding body might mean by empowerment and what a youth worker might mean by empowerment may be very different things, but when a government lays down empowerment as an objective, that creates all sorts of possibilities for interventions in which the young person can be the primary client. The same could be said for inclusion, participation, choice, development, equality/equity, enterprise, opportunity, potential, voice, engagement, learning – most of the buzzwords that constitute youth policy and within which funding decisions are made.

> Intelligent youth work learns the *discourses* that constitute policy and decision-making within governments, bureaucracies or funding bodies, and learns how to reshape them in the interests of young people.

Of course, governments may propose projects that directly confront the rights of young people. Youth curfews, for example, are a common device for policy-makers to 'do something' in the face of the popular fear of young people and concerns about public order. In some situations youth workers have been recruited (and funded) as part of curfew provisions to enable the legal exercise of the curfew, for example by taking over custody of young people who have been removed from the street. Given the profound violation of young people's human and civil rights that curfews constitute, and how deeply prejudicial they are, it is as difficult to justify the participation of youth workers in youth curfews as it is to justify the participation of medical practitioners in the administration of the death penalty. Youth workers should always be clear about the funding that they would say 'no' to.

Conclusion

Things have got a little less flexible over the last decade or so. Governments have become more adept at managing community organisations, invoking a range of techniques and devices of governance, such as strategic planning, competitive tendering, more detailed funding agreements, the specification of outcomes and their measurement through key performance indicators, and a range of other tools borrowed and adapted from business and the market. Initial attempts were mostly fairly clumsy and very open, but governments have sharpened these instruments over time, and the space for independent youth work has been shrinking as a result. There is more money around, but it is more tightly controlled (Davies and Merton 2009).

Governments have also increasingly recognised the potential of youth work-type methods to reach 'hard to serve' people and to address a range of social problems. As a result, there has been a proliferation of support for interventions that look like youth work but don't necessarily carry youth work assumptions and commitments. The Connexions service in England and Wales, the configuration of Community Learning and Development in Scotland, and the increasing engagement of youth workers (or 'youth engagement officers') in schools in Australia are examples. In each of these examples, there can be elements which would be unethical for youth workers (such as a requirement of open access or shareability of a young person's information or penalties for non-attendance) or core commitments which are absent (such as the commitment to voluntary participation or to the young person as the primary client). The extent of government investment in programmes like these could potentially mean that there really isn't any other game in town: if youth workers want to work, they need to work in the Programme, or if they want to be funded, they need to be funded under the Programme.

There isn't an easy answer to this. Youth work commits itself to the young person as the primary client, in their social context. In practice, the amount of space for youth work to be done (even within positions which are designated youth work positions) can be limited. Youth workers can find themselves exploited, and their traditions and skills bastardised in the service of the containment and control of young people. It can end up being difficult to argue that anything that we do is youth work, under this definition, and that the definition is merely aspirational rather than a working conception of youth work in practice.

But the definition also challenges versions of youth work that are about the control of young people, and continues to affirm young people as subjects within the practice of youth work (people who do things) rather than merely objects (people you do things to). It names a practice which may only be defined in the breach: 'I am a youth worker, but this work I am doing is not youth work.' As such, it maintains a *consciousness* of what youth work is. It calls youth workers to be ambitious, to continue to struggle to find a space within which developmental, liberatory, transformative youth work can be done, to find funding sources which will allow enough space for this to happen, and to challenge the structures that prescribe current provision. Fortunately, at this point in time, the possibilities for this are still very open.

Things to consider

- If we knowingly make statements which have a particular meaning for us but we know that a funding body will probably understand a different meaning, isn't that the same as lying anyway?
- What about *evading* the requirements of funding bodies? For example, a funding body might specify that its funds are not to be used for paying for wages, only for capital goods (they do this generally to prevent having to deal with the consequences of staff having to be laid off when a project ends), but extra staff time might be exactly what is needed to make your project fly. Is it OK to use creative accounting (e.g. by overcharging for costs like rent or equipment hire on the project) to move money around so that eventually it becomes available for wages, even though the funder has specified that it shouldn't be?

10

REFERRAL AND WORKING ACROSS PROFESSIONAL DISCIPLINES

Summary

Internationally, there has been increasing pressure for different professions to work together. This a good thing: young people deserve to have the best expertise available when they need it, and youth workers need to be well connected and skilled at making the right referral and in working together on issues with other professionals. Other players might speak different professional languages and have different perspectives on their work with young people, and it isn't always easy. And there can be some quite tricky ethical dilemmas that arise…

Partnership and collaboration has developed as a core practice criterion in youth policy over the last decade. It is overtly required in the *Every Child Matters* (Chief Secretary to the Treasury 2003) and *Youth Matters* (Secretary of State for Education and Skills 2005) policy frameworks in England and *Working and Learning Together* in Scotland (Scottish Executive 2004), but is now standard wherever you look, and youth work services usually have to be able to demonstrate how they are collaborating with other agencies and professions in order to demonstrate that they are meeting 'best practice'. It isn't just in youth work either: collaboration is also in fashion internationally, with schools, universities, government departments and even private businesses needing to demonstrate that they are working with other people.

Collaboration goes by a number of names, such as interdisciplinary, interprofessional, inter-agency, partnership or 'joined up' working (we'll use interdisciplinary), and involves a number of challenges. Some of these challenges are pragmatic in nature: it can be difficult to get interdisciplinary practice to work well (Huxham and Vangen 2000). That's not really the focus of this chapter. We're concerned here with the *ethical* challenges involved in taking on a third party in the youth work relationship.

As for all professions, the youth work role is limited. We cannot, and do not, provide all the things a young person needs, and neither should we aspire to. The power of the professional relationship, across the professions, lies exactly in the limited nature of the relationship, in the expertise that can be developed within this narrow sphere, and the clarity of the focus of attention. It creates problems too. People do not neatly divide up into biological, financial, emotional and spiritual bits, and there is always a tension between holistic and specialist practice. Indeed, the mandate of some professions, like social work and youth work, is to try to bring some of those disparate bits together (Frost et al. 2005); youth work is generalist (or holistic, if you prefer) in nature (Merton et al. 2004).

But to the extent that we are able to do this, we can't also be specialists. The narrowness of our field is precisely that we are generalists. Other professions – police, social workers, psychologists, teachers, careers and guidance personnel, community nurses, doctors, lawyers, physiotherapists, drug counsellors, pastors, psychiatrists, union representatives, community developers, town planners, even architects and engineers on occasion, as well as parents, other family, neighbours, shopkeepers, sports coaches and facility managers – all of these can be really important in the lives of young people, even if (and sometimes because) the young person is not their primary client.

This is a roundabout way of saying that young people need more than youth workers. If young people are going to be able to sort out the issues that prevent them moving forward, they will need connecting up with other people.

Examples of this kind of practice include:

1. **Referral**. Recognising that our knowledge and skill base (and our access to resources, sometimes including time!) is limited, we introduce the young people we are working with to other people who might be useful. For example, a young person might feel their employer has been cheating them on their wages and need to talk to an industrial advocate. Or they have disclosed childhood abuse of some kind, which they feel is affecting their ability to function, so referral to a therapist or psychologist is called for. Or they have heard that the police are after them and need a referral to a lawyer.

2. **Partnership (or multiprofessional or inter-agency) working on issues**. Coming together with a common concern about an issue such as unemployment or teenage pregnancy or urban regeneration, people from a range of organisations and professions work together to try to get things to change. So, a range of people, perhaps coordinated by a government-employed community development officer or a local community activist, is pulled together to get a community centre built or to do something about the increasing amount of drug dealing that seems to be going on within the community.

3. **Interprofessional teams**. A range of professionals work together to try to help a person or group of people who face multiple difficulties or who have to be involved with a number of different services (such as

health, employment, justice and education). This situation is not that uncommon. For example, a young person may have a heavy involvement with drug use and a diagnosed mental illness, and may also be in and out of homelessness.

Things to consider

All of the codes of ethics for youth work we have considered include an ethical requirement for cooperation or collaboration. It is interesting that so many codes have found it necessary to include this provision – and not just youth work codes either. It reflects a tendency for professions to be jealous about their clients, and to be reluctant to see them go off and build relationships with others. It is easy for professions to see their training, knowledge, expertise, discourses and practice as superior to that of other professions, and to doubt whether another profession can make any real difference to the situation – often because they don't really understand it (Irvine et al. 2002; Frost et al. 2005). Is that true of youth workers as well?

Ethical complexities in interdisciplinary work

While collaboration is an ethical requirement, it isn't ethically simple. Our society generally has a pathological view of young people, which often results in young people being treated badly (Wyn and White 1997; Bessant et al. 1998). The professions are not immune from that perspective. Indeed, on occasion they have actively promoted it (Sercombe 1996). Working with or referring young people to professionals who have a prejudicial, paternalistic or pathological view of young people means that we may be exposing a young person to yet another abusive encounter, this time indirectly at our hands. Our responsibility doesn't end when we hand over the phone to a young person to speak to a colleague, or when we have fixed the date for our next inter-agency meeting.

Active referral

There is a balance here between trusting our colleagues to do what they do and the reality that young people often don't fare that well in professional encounters. Or indeed, that professionals don't necessarily fare that well in encounters with young people. The core principle here is that youth work is a relationship. If we introduce a third party into that relationship, we have some responsibility for the ongoing efficacy of the now broader set of relationships. Of course, if it is clear that everything is going fine, it is absolutely appropriate to withdraw, with the door obviously being left open for the young person to come back to us.

Example

As a good youth worker, you are committed to interprofessional practice. The government mental health officer in your neighbourhood has an important role in the mental health network. She does counselling and referral (access to a psychiatrist is difficult, with a long waiting list), but also is the key decision-maker about who will be offered a place in the only half-way house/respite residential facility in the area (though she doesn't have a direct role in the facility). She has a very poor reputation across a wide range of issues: not keeping appointments, inappropriate comments, seemingly random and capricious decision-making, prejudice against certain kinds of clients. One of the young people in your service is clearly in a difficult place at the moment and needs some respite care at least, and probably for her medication to be reviewed. How do you ethically meet your obligations to this young person? Do you have any obligations to service users other than your client? Should you, for example, be confronting the officer about her practice, suggesting training or supervision, contacting her superior, and/or collecting evidence to support her dismissal?

This raises ethical questions about blind referral, where you refer a young person to someone you don't know and haven't checked out. As a general rule, it is better practice to refer a young person to a person than an organisation. Youth workers need to be good networkers, good information gatherers – and probably good gossips. We need to know who is good and who isn't, who communicates effectively with young people and isn't scared of them, who will need support to effectively serve a young person and who you can confidently leave a young person with knowing they will be fine. It is still often necessary to use professionals who aren't that hip with the young folks, but then a supported referral might be needed, where the youth worker is present (if the young person wants them there) for the first session or couple of sessions or maybe even longer.

Resource files

What does your resource file look like? Does it have names and phone numbers, or just organisational details? Have you got around and met the people you would be referring young people to, and have made an assessment of how much support would be needed to make a referral effective? Is it up to date, and do you make a point of meeting up with new practitioners when they take up their positions? Do you follow up with people you have referred?

You're only as good as your networks!

Working across disciplines

There is a general consensus that interdisciplinary working is easier to talk about than it is to do (Huxham and Vangen 2000). The very nature of the professions is that they have their own discourses, their own knowledges, their own ways of seeing the world and putting the world together (Banks 2004). At its best, this provides a rich melange of ways of seeing things that adds additional perspective, dimension and resources for understanding the problem and finding solutions. However, without time spent in being able to hear what different participants are saying, and being able to translate the specialist languages of each of the professions into some kind of common understanding, it can often be the case that participants don't really even understand each other (Griffiths 2000).

The professions are also not equal in status. This shouldn't make any difference in partnership, but it does (Gunson and Collins 1997; Griffiths 2000; Frost et al. 2005). At their best, interdisciplinary processes bring the range of different knowledges to bear to secure the best outcome for the young person. At their worst, they are a means for dominant agencies or professions to establish control over other practitioners in the situation, to silence alternative voices, and to establish a single form and logic of intervention (Irvine et al. 2002). Youth work, as a new profession, and one that is aligned with a low-status and stigmatised client group, tends to be low on the pecking order (or part of what activists in Ferguslie Park called 'the lowerarchy' (Gunson and Collins 1997: 288)). That can mean that youth workers' contributions aren't valued, their often detailed and strongly situated knowledge is disregarded, and what should be a rich and productive conversation is an exercise in frustration and futility. Not always, because individual youth workers are often impressive and other professionals involved are often gracious, generous and of high personal integrity. But often enough, especially if the worker is young.

> *Example*
>
> A very capable, experienced, tertiary trained youth work colleague had been involved for some time with a young person who was also a ward of the state, had a good relationship with her and had done a lot of work with her. Things weren't necessarily going well for the young person, and her case manager from the Department called a case conference, including education, health, juvenile justice and this colleague. After the initial sharing of information, the youth worker was told 'You can go now. The professionals can take it forward from here.'
> How would you have responded?

In general, this can mean that interdisciplinary work is a long way from what Habermas (1994) would have called an 'ideal speech situation'. Discourse ethics, according to Habermas, involves discussion between equals, open and honest communication, and the commitment to seek consensus (Griffiths 2000). In the absence of these elements, interdisciplinary working can be no more than coerced co-option into what powerful officials were going to do anyway (Gunson and Collins 1997).

Ethical protocols can vary as well (Huxham and Vangen 2000). All professions will have some commitment to confidentiality. But police, teachers and sometimes nurses tend to be much freer with information about young people than doctors, counsellors, psychologists and psychiatrists. Youth workers vary a great deal on this question, often because agency policy does. I have known youth workers who won't give any information, even to tell a young person's friends whether they have seen them, and others who have unilaterally opened their files to police. Establishing understanding on this question, and others, is important. If the groundwork isn't done, you can expect participants either to be frustrated by their partners' secretiveness or incensed at their freedom with someone else's information and disregard for privacy. Government-mandated interdisciplinary work can often require very open access to quite personal information. (We'll talk about how we deal with this in the next chapter.)

So. Working collaboratively with other professionals is absolutely required of ethical practice. But it is also fraught. How to get the best from interdisciplinary working, and avoid the worst?

Establishing your professional identity

Davis (1988) argues that a clear professional identity is essential to effective interdisciplinary practice. It works if you understand clearly who you are, and what your professional mandate is, and what other participants are, and what their professional mandate is. If everybody around the table is secure, then the different voices around the table can much more closely follow Habermas's ideal speech situation. Davis argues that this kind of security is developmental in professionals, and involves a number of levels or stages.

> *Unidisciplinarity*: Feeling confident and competent in one's own discipline.
> *Intradisciplinarity*: Believing that you and fellow professionals in your own discipline can make an important contribution to care.
> *Multidisciplinarity*: Recognising that other disciplines also have important contributions to make.
> *Interdisciplinarity*: Willing and able to work with others in the joint evaluation, planning and care of the [young person].
> *Transdisciplinarity*: Making the commitment to teach and practice with other disciplines across traditional boundaries for the benefit of the [young person]...
>
> (in Hewison and Sim 1998: 311)

A key insight is that ethical interdisciplinary working depends first on unidisciplinarity: on your own confidence and clarity of purpose. If you know who you are, are confident in what you have to contribute, and know who you are there for, then a lot of the ethical problems take care of themselves. Not that it will be easy, but the issues will be clearer. The key here is the core ethical stance of the youth worker: that the young person/people are the primary client.

Example

It is increasingly common for youth workers to be engaged by schools to help young people who are struggling. However, differences of approach with school staff are by no means uncommon. In this instance, a youth worker engaged in a schools programme was experiencing some serious conflict with one of the school's student services staff. This finally came to a confrontation in which the youth worker was accused of being a 'loose cannon' – withholding information, discounting opinions of school staff, lack of accountability. To clear up the conflict, the youth worker and her line manager decided to sort this out...using the code of ethics. They arranged a meeting with student services staff and explained, by citing the code, the behaviour of the youth worker and the responsibilities that this involved. In the process of the conversation, the school based staff realised that they had misjudged the worker: that the worker's behaviour was not that of some rogue element but was embedded in a different, but still coherent, professional discipline. They realised that the worker's position is to be accountable to the young people in the school, which was why she couldn't share information. The school and youth service agreed to draft a Memorandum of Understanding using the Code of Ethics as a basis.

Establishing others' professional identity

In fact, all professionals around the table ought to be able to articulate their professional interest: to lay the cards on the table, so to speak. Hewison and Sim (1998) suggest that codes of ethics might be a useful starting point for doing that. In the sharing of codes of ethics, people should be able to articulate both what is unique to their professional position, and also what values are shared as a basis for collaborative action. Alternatively, members of a partnership could be asked to identify the key defining features of their professional commitment using Koehn's formulation of a profession as constituted by its ethical commitment to serve a vulnerable client group (Koehn 1994).

What is everybody here for?

- Who is your client?
- What is the nature of their vulnerability, from your point of view?
- What is your sphere of activity or practice?
- What kind of transformation are you seeking?

So, social workers share with youth workers a commitment to work with the social context, but the young person is not necessarily their primary client. Doctors and nurses are both committed to healing the body, but doctors do it through pursuing cure, nurses by pursuing care. Psychologists should share with youth workers a commitment to the young person as the primary client, but are interested in their internal thoughts and feelings, rather than their social context. The primary client of the police is the state, and their sphere of activity is to uphold the peace through enforcing the law.

This mix might mean that you may be the only person involved in an interdisciplinary process for whom the young person is the primary client. This might mean that the outcome of decisions, despite your advocacy, is clearly not what the young people or person wanted to happen. I don't think that this necessarily compromises you, as long as within the process you are true to your own ethical commitment. It can be difficult: it may mean that consensus is not possible, and it is hard to be the odd one out. However, if the other members of the team are clear from the beginning that your role is to advocate for the interests of the young people, not necessarily to do what is best for other stakeholders, or to meet consensus, the process can be lively and respectful and produce a better decision than would otherwise have been the case.

Conclusion

Youth workers are often passionate about their practice, about its importance as a way of engaging young people and helping them work through the challenges of life. We are often protective of our practice, in the face of a professional community that often doesn't understand it and can be dismissive of our methods and our knowledge base. Often, the fact that we have not been good at explaining the basis of our practice hasn't helped (Merton et al. 2004). This defensiveness has often meant that youth workers are insular, that they don't play well with others. But flying solo is not ethically an option. We can't provide all the knowledge, skill and resources that a young person needs, and even if we could, it wouldn't be a good idea. The challenge is to create interdisciplinary communities of practice that are open to dialogue, accepting of difference and generous to young people. The danger is that interdisciplinary processes become self-serving, or dominated by the partners with the highest status or the most power. Engaging with interdisciplinary processes takes some maturity, some diplomatic skill, courage to work in the face of sometimes unsympathetic environments, and relentless awareness of our commitment to the young person as the primary client.

Things to consider

- Interdisciplinary practice can take a lot of time, lots of meetings. A youth worker's time, fundamentally, belongs to young people. What are the ethical issues involved in this? Can you think of some principles or processes that might guide you?
- You might be instructed by your manager to be involved in an interdisciplinary process even though the whole philosophy of the intervention runs counter to what you believe about young people, and you can't get a hearing for a young person-centred perspective. Can you think of ways to manage this?
- Requirements for collaborative practice are often accompanied by requirements for youth participation in decision-making. Are these two processes contradictory? Does professionals getting together and making decisions leave any room for young people's effective voice in the decision? How might this be resolved?

11

CONFIDENTIALITY

Summary

Confidentiality is central to the ethics of most of the professions. The logic of this is ancient and compelling. But there are ethical problems in keeping confidences as much as there are in breaking them. In practice, young people's expectation of confidentiality is probably frequently broken. Modern work practices may require that a range of people have access to information. Legislation attempting to counter issues ranging from terrorism to drug use to sexual exploitation may require youth workers to disclose young people's information. This chapter explores the nature of professional confidentiality for youth workers, some of the personal struggles involved, and what the limits of confidentiality might be.

The ethical obligation to keep personal and private information in trust has been there from the day the professions were born. You won't find a clearer expression of it than the Hippocratic Oath, written for medical practitioners in the fourth century BC:

> Whatever I see or hear, professionally or privately, which ought not to be divulged, I will keep secret and tell no one.

(BBC 2003)

The reasons for this commitment are also well established, from duty-based, virtue-based, and consequence-based ethical positions. The classic work by ethicist Sissela Bok (1978) gives a precise account of this. First, the information belongs to the person doing the telling. They give that information to be used for particular purposes, and it isn't ours to do what we like with (which could relate either to a duty or a virtue). Second, the relationship we have with the person, and the care we have for them, precludes disclosing information which might be harmful (consequence-based). It would be disloyal, a betrayal of the nature of the relationship (virtue-based). Third, information is given under the overt or presumed promise that it will held in confidence. To betray a confidence is to break a promise (duty-based).

This would be true of any relationship: a friend, a partner, a business associate. Bok argues that the particular nature of the professional relationship generates an extra level of duty, however. In Chapter 2, we explored the idea of a professional relationship creating a space within which transformation can happen. We argued there that for all of the liberal professions, a commitment to confidentiality protected the space, making it safe for a person to develop trust, and to say what they felt needed to be said, to tell secrets if they needed to, and for them to be protected in the telling. This commitment has been supported by law and convention across time, on consequentialist grounds: it is in society's long-term interest to allow secrets to be told and kept, even where it might have an intense interest (e.g. in the case of major crimes) in the content of the disclosure.

Youth work is no different. The style and context of our work may be different from the other professions, and we have a particular purpose and a particular set of loyalties, but this core dynamic of trust, disclosure and resolution still holds. Because of the long history of the ethics of confidentiality, there are now well-established positions across the professions on 'best practice' regarding confidentiality and its limits (e.g. Royal College of Nursing 2005; British Medical Association 2008). Even in the case of youth work, where writing on ethics is still sparse, Barbara Raiment (1994), Susie Daniel (1997), and Sue Morgan and Sarah Banks (1999) have all engaged in sophisticated analyses. All of the youth work codes of ethics mention confidentiality, with the New Zealand/Aotearoa code (National Youth Workers Network Aotearoa 2008) giving detailed guidance on the practice for youth work.

There is also a body of relevant legislation across Western countries, both in common law and in the statutes (Royal College of Nursing 2005). It is important to be accurately informed about the legal situation in your own setting. As well as not knowing when they have to disclose, youth workers often think they legally have to disclose when they don't. There may be no legal obligation to disclose crimes, for example, or to help police with their inquiries (in the UK at least), provided that you have 'lawful excuse', and confidentiality would count as a lawful excuse (Royal College of Nursing 2005: 18). Legal pressures to disclose are, however, on the increase (Donner et al. 2008).

Youth work and confidentiality: the uncontested bits

The general requirement for youth workers to protect young people's confidential and private information is uncontroversial. Young people's expectation of confidentiality from youth workers is very high, and their sense of betrayal when this is compromised is often intense (Daniel 1997). This is especially so when so many adults in their lives treat them as incapable of making their own decisions and looking after themselves, and can't be trusted not to take things out of their hands. We may be the only person in their lives who they feel they can trust to work with them on issues, or just listen, without going off.

There is also a consensus that this duty is not absolute, that there may be a range of circumstances where disclosure is not only justified, but ethically required. There are some well-established parameters for this: the Aotearoa/New Zealand code of ethics describes them in some detail (National Youth Workers Network Aotearoa 2008). Most youth work organisations and most youth workers will have policies and practices around that, or should have. The limits may vary from context to context and with organisational philosophy, but they should be clear, written down, readily accessible, and known backwards. The policy should be clear and open about whether the undertaking is to keep confidentiality strictly to the youth worker to whom the disclosure is made, or to that person and their supervisor, or within the team (i.e. the team is informed, but will not speak of it to anyone outside the team). In that case, you have to be really clear about who the team is, especially if you are using volunteers or sessional youth workers.

Communicating the limits to confidentiality

The issue then (given the informal environment of most of our work) is how you can communicate these limits to the young person so that they fully understand the implications of telling you their story. The Australian code of ethics says that:

> Information provided by young people will not be used against them, nor will it be shared with others who may use it against them. Young people should be made aware of the contextual limits to confidentiality, and their permission sought for disclosure. Until this happens, the presumption of confidentiality must apply.

> (Youth Affairs Council of Western Australia 2003: 11)

In other words, young people have a right to expect that any confidential communication will stay confidential, and any private information will stay private, unless you have been really clear about the exceptions. We engage young people in a deception and a betrayal if we do not do our best to communicate the truth of our pledge of confidentiality beforehand.

Leaflets or posters are one way of doing that. For programmes that have a clear point of entry, explanation of the confidentiality business could be part of the welcoming or induction process. It is a bit harder with 'open door' activities, and even more with detached work. Many young people may have quite a casual or even incidental contact with the service: they might just happen to be on the street or the park where you are working or come to a dance party you have organised. It would be impossible to have a chat with every young person in a half-mile radius about what their rights to confidentiality and its limitations are. This isn't a problem for a psychologist, when they come to your rooms at an appointed time and you open a file on them. As youth workers, we need good process as well as some kind of trigger or threshold so we know when the process needs to be kicked off. A clear contracting process is one way to do that.

Contracting and the client relationship

We have found it useful in practice to distinguish between different kinds of relationships that we have with young people because the ethical obligation is different in different kinds of relationships. The language may or may not appeal, but the core distinction may be useful in being clearer about our relationship and the ethical obligations engendered by it.

One way to handle this is to distinguish between:

- *contacts* (e.g. a young person who you have seen around and may know the name of but haven't really had a serious conversation with)
- *customers* (e.g. a young person may just want to be a part of a basketball game or come to an event organised by the service) and
- *clients* (where a more intensive relationship is involved, such as where there is counselling or advocacy).

Each of these relationships involves certain obligations and duties of care, and there are elements of the professional relationship which apply even to our relationship with young people we have never met. Any young person is a potential client, and needs to be afforded professional protections as part of that, and we have ethical obligations to young people as a population as well as to individuals and groups.

However, a specific professional relationship is invoked at the point where a customer becomes a client, with all the limits and protections of that. A minimum standard is the point at which there is *disclosure with the invitation to intervene*. As we discussed in Chapter 3, this may not always be verbal, the invitation may not be explicit, and the circumstances in which it arises may be ambiguous and hard to pick, so this isn't a silver ethical bullet. It can still be tricky. But at the very least, at the point of disclosure with the invitation to intervene, the young person should know as unambiguously as possible what you are offering in the youth work relationship and what you aren't.

So, at or before the point where the young person becomes a client, we will, wherever possible, spell out the nature of our contract with them. This might include telling them about:

- the agency, including the sponsoring organisation, our sources of funding and the objectives of the agency
- our confidentiality policy
- the nature of referral
- the need for record keeping and what records will be kept
- the policy of the young person as the primary client
- how to complain if our work is not satisfactory
- how to dismiss us and engage another youth worker or youth service.

It may be possible to convey all of this information before this, maybe as part of some sort of induction workshop for new members or in freely accessible literature. It might not be appropriate to do it all at once. You might want to spread it over several conversations, though the confidentiality conversation is imperative before disclosure happens.

When the promise of confidentiality needs to be broken

The framework above covers the general circumstances of disclosure. The slightly trickier question is when a situation doesn't fall into the clear limitations you or your agency has anticipated, but where it is clear that you have some duty which contradicts your obligation to confidentiality. This happens all the time, with varying strengths. Added to this is a doubt, often unfounded but sometimes not, about young people's developmental capacity to make wise decisions or give informed consent, which can mean that the right thing to do is to take control out of their hands. Some examples, many of them factual, are given below.

Examples

1. You are working as a detached youth worker, talking to a couple of young people at a park bench. Just the other side of the bench, a group of three or four young people you don't know very well is discussing a particular house that would be very easy to break into. You know the house. A couple of days later, you find out that the house the young people were describing was burgled. What should you do?

2. A young person you know seems to have gone up in the world. They left school early and were unemployed for a time. They have reappeared recently, more confident, better dressed and have a profile among the other young people in the area, including those who come to your service. The young people tell you the person is dealing drugs. A drug-based lifestyle is a definite risk for the young people you are working with. Do you have any responsibility to act?

3. You are out and about in the neighbourhood and the police cruise by. They stop and ask if you have seen a particular young person. You have – about five minutes ago. You also know where the young person said they were going and where they are living at the moment. What do you say?

4. A young person takes the opportunity of a quiet moment to ask if he can talk to you about something and if you will keep it in confidence. You say yes, as long as he isn't intending to hurt himself or anyone else. He says no, he doesn't want to hurt anybody, but he feels bad about something that happened in the past. You take him to a quiet room. He then tells you in some detail of a horrific rape that he committed four years earlier. What should you do? What obligation do you have to the girl he raped?

5. A mother storms into the youth centre, furious. She has just found out that her 15 year-old daughter has had an abortion. She also found out that the

daughter had talked to you about the pregnancy and what to do about it, and you had phoned the family planning clinic and helped her make an appointment. The mother would have been quite happy to help raise the child. Does she have a right to be angry?

6. Your agency is involved in a joint piece of work with the police, aiming to reduce tensions between young people, other shoppers and shopkeepers in a local shopping centre. The police have given you a wealth of insight into the young people's lives from a copper's point of view, including family histories that you didn't know about. They haven't pushed it yet, but they will also want some reciprocity here. What kind of information would you be willing to give them?

These cases are hard. Fundamentally, it is not good to have to work this out on your own. You need access to wise heads and hearts: to a supervisor or trusted colleagues. This can be negotiated with the young person when you discuss the limits to confidentiality in the first place. Unfortunately, what your colleagues recommend ethically, or even insist upon, can't be foreseen and therefore are not negotiated. Our commitment to the young person as the primary client doesn't go away, and we need to keep fighting for it. But sometimes countervailing interests weigh very heavily indeed.

The case of child protection

Much of the recent conversation about youth work and confidentiality has revolved around legal obligations to report allegations of neglect or physical, emotional or sexual abuse of young people, or suspicion of such abuse or neglect. In fact, the child protection apparatus is almost overwhelming, and questioning its assumptions is difficult. Susie Daniel has given this matter close attention (Daniel 1997), and it plays a central role in Morgan and Banks' (1999) chapter as well. Most organisations have child protection policies in place and governmental guidance on the matter is immense, so we won't spend so much time on it here.

On the face of it, however, the legal requirement to report contradicts the requirement for confidentiality, unless that limit has been communicated to the young person. This demonstrates all the classical reasons why confidentiality is protected among the professions. If the young person is frightened about the consequences (and Susie Daniel's work indicates they have a right to be), they may be left completely isolated. As it is, starting up the mandatory reporting process may well prompt the young person to retract allegations, at the risk of great personal damage, when they find out (Daniel 1997).

In most English-speaking countries, action is sought through the criminal justice system, and while this is sometimes what a young person wants, often they just want the behaviour to stop, especially if it is a family member who is the perpetrator. The record of authorities in achieving a result that is better for the young person through the joint operations of the justice and welfare systems isn't that reassuring. Daniel quotes a poignant poem written by a 12 year-old about her experience:

> I asked you to put an end to the abuse
> You put an end to my whole family
> You took away my nights of hell
> And gave me days of hell instead
> You've exchanged my private nightmare
> For a very public one.

(Daniel 1997: 4)

The poem has another ten verses like that. It isn't the experience of every young person, and doing nothing in a situation that is abusive can amount to collusion – you becoming a kind of silent partner in the abuse. Even when the young person doesn't want you to do anything, doing nothing is not an option.

This is the thing about confidentiality. Being involved in a secret brings you into the circle of the secret: you become in some way part of the picture. (It is partly why sexual abuse, with its terrible weight of secrecy, is so cruel. It implicates the victim in their own abuse.) This can be a heavy emotional weight for a youth worker. Building some place for you to offload your secrets, to a supervisor, partner or confidante, is an important mechanism for gaining perspective and balance (see Chapter 21). Some youth workers, on the other hand, thrive on secrets, seeking out disclosures from young people and cherishing them as evidence of their ability to connect with young people and win their trust, finding endorsement there for themselves as workers and as people. There is potential for corruption here (see Chapter 17).

Not all early sexual experience is experienced by young people as abusive, though the law sees it that way (Daniel 1997). In such cases, the movement of the situation through the welfare and criminal justice systems into the public sphere can be devastating. Young people can be caught up in a range of intrusive, difficult, often public and sometimes incompetent processes driven by people they do not know and in which they have no control. The question of consent, or whether the event is experienced as abusive or unpleasant or exploitative, isn't generally seen as relevant.

While I have worked extensively with young people who have been abused or exploited sexually, and even more who have been neglected, I have thankfully never been in the position where I have had to mandatorily report. The existence of such a requirement would not, for me at least, mean that I would necessarily comply, especially not immediately (Donner et al. 2008). While the law is always a factor in ethical consideration, *ethics does not automatically require that you obey the law*. In this case, my obligation to the young person as my primary client, along with a range of other ethical commitments to confidentiality, duty of care and promoting empowerment, weigh heavier than my obligation to the law.

This is not easy to say. The abuse of a young person, sexual, emotional or physical, is a great evil. If I could be convinced that the young person would fare well within the statutory processes, that they would be consulted about what would happen to them, that their wishes would be heard and given priority, then the very great dilemma that such a situation involves would be lightened. Sadly, there are enough instances of this not being the case to prevent me taking it for granted (Daniel 1997). In the absence of such reassurance, my commitment is to the young person with whom I am working, and the ethical struggles involved are my responsibility. When faced with such a situation, however, whatever my decision, it is never an option to do nothing.

Conclusion

Confidentiality is one of the primary ethical principles of most of the caring professions, including youth work. However, it is also one of the most problematic. In practice, confidentiality is compromised routinely by everyday practices within youth work agencies, and young people's expectation of confidentiality is probably frequently broken. Youth workers need to be clear about what they mean when they offer confidentiality, and the limits of the offer should be clear to young people, preferably before significant interaction takes place.

12

YOUTH WORKERS, SEX AND YOUNG PEOPLE

Summary

It has been normal for all of the professions to control the sexual dimensions of the professional relationship and to exclude sexual engagement from the professional encounter. There are good reasons for this. Aside from the betrayal of the professional commitment that it involves, such relationships are very frequently damaging. However, while the most overt forms of sexual exploitation might be obvious, there are a number of situations in youth work where the ethics are a little more complex, such as the situation with volunteers or with young people who may not have a strong link to the youth service, and whether we have a role in intervening in the sex lives of young people we work with.

Sex is one of the most controversial areas of ethical decision-making. For most people, and in most societies, sex is not just a physical act, like walking or eating. It is deeply relational. It is also deeply connected to structures of desire, which make it a strong element in the dynamics of power. As a physical act, for most people it is also wired into our emotional structures and responses, which can range from sublime happiness to foul jealousy to hopeless despair (Scruton 2001). So it cannot be anything but infused with ethical questions.

Rules about under what conditions sexual relations are permissible have been a feature of most human communities – I have never heard of a society that had no rules about sex. Different societies have insisted on different standards: some have been monogamous, others polygamous; some have allowed extra-marital sexual activity as long as it is discreet; some have seen homosexuality as an abomination, others, in certain circumstances, obligatory (Schnapp 1997).

For most societies, the connection of sex to the birth of children has shaped their ethical systems. Reproduction is crucial for any society, and the circumstances of the birth and upbringing of children are important not only for children to be well cared for, but for a society to be healthy and for generational succession to be secure. In our society, with the introduction of reliable and convenient contraception, the nexus between sex and conception has been broken. With it, the ethical responsibility to provide a proper relationship environment for the arrival of a baby is no longer built into the ethics of the sex act. There has also been a much wider awareness, due to travel, social mobility and education, of the variety of sexual experience and the variety of cultural ethical norms. As a result, the last 40 years has seen a wide liberalisation of sex, with a profound decoupling of sex from marriage and a range of experiments in the form of sexual relationships as well as actual sexual practices. The growth of the internet has added to this, both in terms of free and anonymous voyeuristic participation in an unlimited range of sexual acts, and a fluid means of finding and connecting with potential sexual partners.

In this environment, it is no longer clear how we should live sexually. And yet, as any day's reading of the tabloid newspapers or the celebrity magazines will demonstrate, sex is just as laden with ethical decisions and ethical judgements as it has ever been (including the ethics of making ethical judgements about sex). There does seem to be a persistent conviction, shared across a number of different cultures, that 'sex implicates a … [person's] innermost being and constitutive aspects' (Belliotti 1993; Carmody 2009a) – or, slightly more familiarly, '...don't you understand? You take me by the heart when you take me by the hand' (Chapman and Chinn 1982). According to ethicists like Punzo (1969) and Scruton (2001), careless sexual activity dehumanises people and 'threatens their existential integrity', regardless of what ideologies they may hold about sex. This is the position routinely held by natural law ethicists as well, who argue that human beings are designed to live within a certain code of sexual practice.

But what code? A number of religious traditions sanction relationships within which sex is approved (typically, in the West, lifetime heterosexual marriage). But that doesn't help if you aren't committed to that tradition, and in most Western societies, that is most people. In addition, the Marxist critique of 'bourgeois morality' and the feminist critique of the relationship between sex and power have both demonstrated that many of the traditional codes perpetuated male dominance, oppressed women and people who weren't heterosexual, and restricted sexual expression and fulfilment even in 'approved' relationships.

Sex, contract and the consenting adult

In secular societies, sexual ethics has mostly been grounded in ideas of contract. Sex and the terms of a sexual relationship (such as not sleeping with anyone else while you are in that relationship) are a matter of agreement. If you don't want to get hurt, you work through the agreement carefully to make sure your expectations and the expectations of your partner match. It is up to you, and no one else, to protect your 'constitutive aspects'. The only rule, then, for sexual practice is *consent*: the contract, to be valid, needs to have been entered into without force or fraud (Belliotti 1993; Carmody 2009a). There should be sufficient communication for each person to understand what is being agreed to, but again that is nobody's responsibility but the people concerned.

Our attention then shifts to the nature of consent. Real consent cannot be given where a person cannot realistically say 'no'. For example, when:

- the power difference between the parties is large
- one party is so desperate that they do not really have a choice (e.g. they may be starving or their children need medicine)
- they are in no position to understand the contract (e.g. children and some people with learning disabilities)
- either party's decision-making is compromised by alcohol or other drugs.

While this is the *de facto* position in the absence of a consensus about sexual ethics, it by no means solves all the problems. For example, a sexual relationship, for many people, involves a range of feelings, responses and attachments which they did not necessarily anticipate. Can you contract adequately without knowing what the journey will entail? Scruton (2003) argues that in sex, you give your*self* to another, and that giving your*self* is an act of trust, of putting yourself is someone else's hands. Contract is an inadequate vehicle to carry that kind of relationship. (See also William May's (1975) argument about contract versus covenant in Chapter 2.)

Consent is not black and white, either/or. There are degrees of consent between enthusiastic, informed agreement, on the one hand, and outright refusal on the other. Think about arranged marriages, for example. It is possible to 'kind of' consent, or to not 'not' consent, and it isn't necessarily clear where the line is for an 'adequate' level of consent. Some radical feminists have argued that given the power difference between men and women, all heterosexual sex is coerced (Johnston 1974; Bunch 1987). On the other hand, VanRee argues that sex with children is ethical as long as the child initiates and is free to remove themselves from the situation when they want to (VanRee 1999). This is not a position many of us would share.

Issue 1: On sex between youth workers and young people

Most professions have a blanket embargo on sexual relations with clients. Indeed, for some professional groups in the USA, it is a criminal offence to engage sexually with a client, or even a former client (Corey et al. 2007). There isn't a lot that has been published about youth workers and sexual relationships with young people – it doesn't appear in the index of any of the major texts on youth work or youth work ethics and I could find no references in the journals either. Yet this is a real issue for youth workers. In an equivalent study in another profession, Pope and his colleagues found that only 77 out of 585 therapists they surveyed reported never having been sexually attracted to their clients (Corey et al. 2007). Given our demographic, the figure is unlikely to be lower for youth workers. Yet guidance on how to manage their desire is scant. The codes of ethics are mostly clear, but their reach is still uneven across different constituencies, and the degree to which they are seen as compelling varies. Many constituencies do not, at this time, have a code of ethics.

Why is sex with a young person unethical?
The logic of power difference

A common standard for determining whether sexual relationships are ethical or not is to do with the power difference between the two parties. When the sexual initiator is a powerful person, the respondent may not feel that he or she is really able to refuse and so real consent cannot be granted. This tends to be the standard reason why sex with young people – and, indeed, sexual contact across the professions – is discouraged (Hall 2001). This is also the reason why paedophilia and incest are also seen as illegitimate. Logically then, if a youth worker has significantly more power than the young person, it would not be acceptable, but if there was a small power difference (e.g. if the youth worker and the young person are a similar age) or none at all, it might be OK.

The capacity of a person to give full and free consent to a sexual engagement is obviously important (Belliotti 1993). However, I don't think the 'power difference' argument is enough by itself to support an ethic of sexual relationships between youth workers and young people. For example:

1. All relationships involve power differences of some kind. How big a power difference is too big for an ethical sexual encounter to take place? And who decides?
2. Power is neither consistent nor stable. People can be powerful in one area of their life but subordinate in another. A tiger at work can be a pussy cat at home. Power balances also shift over time: your perfectly equal partner could have a stroke or lose their job. A powerful person can be completely dominated by the person they desire, regardless of their status.
3. Power itself is sexually exciting for many people, and it may be the less powerful person who is initiating a sexual encounter for that reason. It is not unusual for people to choose a sexual partner, male or female, *because* they are powerful, or rich, or intelligent, or have a dominant personality. Situations where less powerful people will eagerly agree to, or initiate, a relationship with a more powerful person are neither rare nor improper. Winning the sexual attention of a powerful person is itself a source of power.
4. While the structural position, training and perhaps age of the youth worker is certainly a source of power, power comes in many forms and from many places (including sexual attractiveness). There are some extremely powerful young people around, and some not very powerful youth workers. In order to work with this criterion, you would need an actual assessment of the relative power of the youth worker and the young person. On the basis of this calculation, a sexual relationship could be approved or not. Intuitively, this does not seem right.

Never acceptable?

I don't think that sexual engagement with a young person who is a client of yours, or even a potential client, is *ever* acceptable. The logic of this is not to do with power difference but to do with the nature of the relationship. In Chapter 2, we argued that the youth work relationship is a professional relationship, which is intentionally limited in order to create a space within which a young person can explore their emerging adulthood. Like sexual relationships, the youth work relationship involves trust: a young person feels able to put themselves in the hands of a youth worker, confident that the youth worker will act in their interest. This trust creates intimacies: we know things about young people, potentially, that no one else knows, and know the young person in ways that no one else knows them. Young people are prepared for us to know these things because they believe they can trust not only the information but *themselves* with us.

It does not take effort for this kind of intimacy to take on an erotic quality. That can happen quite naturally. Hall (2001) argues that the development of desire in professional relationships, through the process of transference, is almost normal. Transference is a process whereby someone projects on to you feelings that are really to do with their own process and their own journey. They may well see you as an ideal person, a liberator, someone really special (see Corey et al. 2007: 44–52). This can be productive, giving the young person the courage or permission to move on to the next part of the journey. It also makes you more attractive than you would otherwise be.

If you are good at what you do, if the relationships you build with young people are transformative, some of them will fall in love with you. But to allow the relationship to move in sexual directions exploits an intimacy which had a different purpose, and which held a promise that it would be protected from the complications and mixed motives of sexual demand. It is a betrayal of that promise. More than that, it means that the relationship is now no longer available for the purpose for which it was entered into. The young person no longer has access to their youth worker because their youth worker is no longer a youth worker. The relationship is no longer about them, as a professional relationship should be. They have lost that.

Sex with a young person you are working with, then, isn't wrong (just) because of a power difference. It is wrong because it is a professional relationship, and the professional relationship carried an (at least implicit) guarantee that it would not be carried over into sexual engagement, *even if that is what the young person would want*. Sexual involvement makes the original engagement a lie, and is a fundamental betrayal of your commitment as a youth worker. If the experience of other professions is any indication, it is also almost always harmful (Bouthoutsos et al. 1983).

But what if the young person is not a client?

Things are slightly more complicated when you don't really have a professional relationship with a young person and something starts to develop. If a person you fancy happens to be under 25, but has no youth work connection with you, I don't see a problem (all things being equal) unless you are using your youth work skills for predatory purposes. If you met the person in a youth work context, but the contact was not significant, things might be a bit more ambiguous.

> ## Example
>
> Mark, 19, is a part-time youth worker in a community arts programme. Roseanne, also 19, comes to the programme once, but it is not really her thing, partly because most of the participants are much younger. Mark, however, is rather more her thing. They happen to meet a week or two later at the shops and exchange phone numbers.
>
> - Is Roseanne a 'young person'?
> - Is she Mark's client, or just a customer or contact? (see Chapter 11). Does it make a difference?
> - Should Mark have given Roseanne his phone number?
> - What should Mark do now?
> - If you were Mark's manager, what would you do?

A past client?

Many professions set a time within which it is not permissible to have a relationship with a past client: usually two years. Youth work traditions are not well established on these fronts. According to Hall (2001), there is no evidence that the problem of transference is diminished by the passage of time. She claims that for doctors at least (and I can think of no reason why youth workers would be any different) the relationship is always infused with the quality of the professional encounter (Hall 2001).

A colleague? A student or trainee? The parent or sibling of a young person?

None of the codes prohibits a relationship developing with a colleague, though it can get messy if things don't work out. The situation is obviously more difficult with a volunteer youth worker, a youth work student, or where a colleague was once a client. The critical question is: is there a professional relationship here, even if it isn't a youth work relationship? If there is, as there often is between student and mentor, for example, I think a sexual relationship is excluded. Note that the North American code also prohibits a relationship with a family member, which is particularly important in residential care and other situations where we work with a young person's parents (Mattingly 1995).

If in doubt, talk. Individuals are not good at dealing with these matters alone. Desire is prone to find its own justifications, and dealing properly with a situation after desire has been allowed to engage is difficult. In situations where guidance from the profession is not well established, it is important for youth work organisations to frame their own positions. For all of us, it is important to talk with trusted colleagues if a potential relationship has its origins in our professional practice. Before we get on the train.

Issue 2: On using your sexuality to get what you want

We noted above that sexuality was a form of power. Sexual attractiveness can be a means of getting people to do what you want: people want to help people who are sexy, want to be closer to them, want to be liked by them, even if they have no real ambition for an actual sexual encounter. In youth work, there are a number of scenarios that could emerge about the use of sexuality to get what you want.

Example

A coordinator of a youth centre is applying, in a competitive tendering process, for a grant to provide a youth service. The coordinator is a very attractive person. They invite the government bureaucrat responsible for short-listing tenders for the service to the youth centre to show them how the centre runs and to see the set-up. In the period up to the granting of the tender, the bureaucrat and the coordinator meet several times, although no physical contact ensues.

- How do you judge the coordinator's action ethically?
- Does it make a difference if the coordinator is a man or a woman? Why?
- Is the coordinator illegitimately and unfairly making use of a personal resource (their sexuality) which is not available to the coordinator of another service, who may be competent but unattractive? Or can a coordinator use whatever resources are available to them in the interests of the young people they work with?

Issue 3: On interventions into the sexual behaviour of young people you work with

The youth work literature explores a range of interventions into young people's sexual lives. However, these interventions are almost all concerned with sexual health and the possibility of transmitting disease, interventions around sexual violence, and interventions under child protection mandates. Given the lack of a consensus about sexual ethics, this is a really tricky area. However, if we are really concerned with young people's development, especially their emotional and social development, we are also concerned with their sexual development – especially its ethics. In Moira Carmody's research (Carmody and Willis 2006;

Carmody 2009a), young people indicated that pretty much everyone had vacated the field of sexual ethics with young people, leaving them with no guidance as how to make ethical decisions about sex, and finding out only at their own cost and the cost of people they had hurt (Carmody and Willis 2006).

Example

A colleague recently reported the practice of 'daisy chaining' among girls they were working with. Daisy chaining is a kind of sexual competition between girls (these were about 12 years old) about how many boys they can have sex with in a single night.

In a recent television programme, there was an interview with a group of 16 year-old boys about regular 'spa nights'. They would contact a girl over the internet and invite them around to one of their parents' houses to have sex with all the boys in the group (while the parents were out). Expectations seemed openly discussed and the encounter seemed consensual.

A sexual health intervention is obviously called for here. Is an ethical health intervention also required? Are these young people's 'constitutive aspects' at risk?

Other situations you might think about:
In a youth centre or club:

- Explicit sexual talk or joking.
- Young people accessing pornography on agency computers.
- A boyfriend and girlfriend wanting to share a tent on a camp. They may routinely share a bed at home.
- Pornographic magazines in a youth accommodation service. The owner may be quite discreet with them.

The standard approach by most youth services seems to be to prohibit any of these forms of sexual expression by young people. Certainly, that makes it easier for us. However, by doing so, do we eliminate opportunities to work with young people around the development of their sexual ethics?

In detached youth work settings, where the behavioural ground rules are not set by you and you don't have the option of prohibiting anything, things can be even more challenging. For example:

- Young people who are working as prostitutes
- Young people who are vulnerable to sexual exploitation, or who are in the process of being exploited because of intoxication or homelessness or poverty
- Discussions of sexual encounters which may be exploitative or violent, with the young people either as the passive or active party.

Many of these situations are normal for young people on the street, and young people themselves may be quite relaxed or blasé about them. They may reflect situations where young people are being exploited sexually. But they may also involve situations in which young people are the exploiters.

Kerry Young argues that 'the challenge for youth work is how to develop a practice that ... supports young peoples' disposition towards virtue: as a central dimension of their self-esteem; and as social beings in a morally textured land-scape' (Young 2006: 45). This surely includes sexual virtue. In the absence of any consensus about sexual ethics, and in the ongoing shadow of a range of repressive traditions about sex, this work is difficult. Even to talk of sexual virtue is confronting. But then, most of our work is. Moira Carmody has identified education in sexual ethics as essential to addressing sexual violence as well as general well-being (Carmody 2009a; see also Carmody 2009b).

Conclusion

This chapter has not laid out an ethics of sexuality for youth workers. On some matters, such as sexual relationships between youth workers and young people, as a profession we are now pretty clear. We have seen the damage done, and despite differences in our own personal sexual ethics, we have found a consensus. On others, such as our role in helping young people develop their own sexual ethics, we aren't so clear, and there just isn't the space here to work it through systematically. There is little guidance for youth workers who confront what they see as deeply problematic sexual behaviour or attitudes in the lives of young people they work with.

The question of ethics and young people's sexuality is not trivial. If, as Belliotti argues, sex 'implicates a person's most constitutive aspects', then it is time those conversations started to happen.

13

TAKING CARE AND MANAGING RISK

Summary

The concept of duty of care has become a major guiding principle in public life. This chapter outlines the kinds of risks that youth work practice is prone to, and measures for managing those risks. However, not taking risks is also risky, and a major part of good youth work practice is putting young people into risky, but not dangerous, situations.

Entering into the life of another person is a risky business. But it is what we do. We overtly seek to meet young people, and to develop relationships with them: not just because it is nice for them or for us, but because we want to make a difference to the way their life is or will be. To a greater or lesser degree, they put themselves in our hands. Indeed, we work to draw out that kind of relationship, that kind of trust. We work with young people to help shape, or reshape, the kind of person they are, or (within limits) the kind of person they want to be.

This engagement is full of risks. If we get it wrong, we can inhibit, repress, even crush a transformation that is only just beginning, reinforce walls of defensiveness that prevent a young person moving at all, add extra weight to personal histories of exclusion or criticism or neglect or invisibility. We can create inflated expectations that will never be met, and leave young people to manage their own failure or disappointment in the wake.

Beyond the relationship itself, we expose young people to new relationships with other young people that could prove to be destructive. We lead them into activities where they could become injured, perhaps permanently. If we neglect maintenance of buildings, vehicles or equipment, or attention to details such as fire extinguishers, our action or inaction can lead to accidents and perhaps even death. When we create environments for young people to be in, and facilitate relationships in which they engage, all of these risks emerge – and more.

Cheerful prospect, isn't it? Still, these risks need to be taken seriously. There is now a solid tradition of law and custom that makes people liable for their interventions into other people's lives, for the services they provide, or for the goods that they offer. Including youth workers. In law, this responsibility is referred to as *duty of care*. In the traditions of professional ethics, it is known as *non-maleficence*.

Would you like a decomposing snail with your ginger beer, madam?

The landmark legal case about duty of care involved a certain Scottish lady, a Mrs Donoghue, who went for a nice day out with her friend in the summer of 1932. A thirsty day in Paisley it was, but her friend produced a bottle of ginger beer with which to quench their thirst. It wasn't until they got to the bottom of the bottle that they found the decomposing snail...

Well, Mrs Donoghue wasn't very well as a result, and sued. The problem was, however, that she didn't buy the ginger beer, so had no contractual relationship with the manufacturer. No matter, said Lord Atkin, presiding:

> You must take reasonable care to avoid acts or omissions which you can reasonably foresee would be likely to injure your neighbour. Who, then, in law is my neighbour? ... [P]ersons who are so closely and directly affected by my act that I ought reasonably to have them in contemplation.

> (in Conde 2004: 29)

Donoghue v. Stevenson established a legal rule, and in the process clarified an ethical one. As John Donne would have said, we are not islands, entire of ourselves. We are parts of communities, our actions impact on other people, and we are responsible for those actions if they are likely to cause injury. This responsibility extends to all our neighbours, not just young people. If we play music at a youth centre loud and late into the night in a built-up residential neighbourhood, we are responsible for our neighbours' lack of sleep and need to do what we can to minimise it. Even more, if we are directly providing something – a service, an experience, some equipment, a venue, a space – it is our responsibility to make sure that people are not harmed by it. Or more accurately, to foresee what would be likely to injure, and make sure that the risk of such injury is minimised.

Non-maleficence and *primum non nocere*

The principle of non-maleficence goes back at least to the Hippocratic Oath, which requires the physician to 'help the sick to the best of my ability and judgement' and to 'abstain from harming or wronging any man' (BBC 2003). This is an undertaking beyond the ethical duty of any good person to avoid injury to their neighbour. The obligation arises from the special position given to the professional, the privileged access that is given to people's personal lives, and the greater opportunity for damage or maliciousness that this involves. A physician might hate the patient, the patient may have wronged them in all sorts of ways, but the physician cannot, ever, act in ways that harm the patient.

That principle has been carried forward into codes of ethics across the professions, including youth work. There isn't any disagreement between the different codes on the need to assess the risks in any programme or practice to avoid doing harm to participants. There is one detail, however, that is more controversial.

The Latin phrase *primum non nocere* literally means 'first (or above all), do no harm'. You will notice that the phrase is carried directly through into the North American standard, as it does in many codes of ethics outside youth work. Gillon (1985) argues that for medicine at least, the principle is not well thought out. The problem is in the 'above all' bit. No one seems to know when that addition was introduced because it wasn't in the Hippocratic Oath. The phrase means that the first responsibility of the professional is to make sure that nothing worse happens to the person than has already happened. For medicine at least, Gillon argues, you cannot promise that. Many medical procedures involve taking risks which may well mean that the person is worse off. You have to make a judgement based on probabilities. This infected foot may kill you. It may not. If it is amputated, it won't, but you will only have one foot. You are worse off with one foot than two, but better off alive than dead.

This is true for youth work as well. Above all, we need to do the best we can to help a young person in their journey. That may involve harm. It may also involve avoiding even greater harm. We don't always know that our assessment of that, even in consultation with the young person, will be accurate.

Example

If a young person is being sexually abused, it is highly likely that reporting it to the authorities will cause further harm to the young person (Daniel 1997). It is also highly likely that continuing sexual abuse will cause further harm. Either way, we cause further harm. Do we report? It is a judgement call. It may not be what the young person wants to do, because they have a good idea of what will happen in their world if they report and not much idea of what compensatory protections might be afforded. Nevertheless, we may find that ethically we *have* to report, given the damage that we can see being done.

Harm is a possibility in almost any intervention that we take with young people: a conversation, a football match, a drug education workshop, a game of pool. The point is to be scrupulous in assessing the risk of harm, to maximise measures which reduce the likelihood of harm, or that minimise the extent of harm should it occur.

Risk and risk management

Beyond ethical codes, the discourse of risk has pervaded every element of modern social life. Ulrich Beck (1992) argues that the production and management of risk is, in fact, the core structural dynamic of late capitalism: that producing enough goods and services is no longer any sort of problem, but that managing the risks of production is. So, from managing environmental damage to political opposition to juggling the balance of debt and assets, the modern economy runs on risk and its management. That's why banks and insurance companies are so important.

Community services of various kinds have taken on the same mantra, especially in the risk to children of sexual abuse, but not only there. Fears of litigation have meant that many agencies (particularly local authorities or large charities which may have assets to plunder) have clamped down heavily on activities which might expose young people to some possibility of harm, especially water-based activities. A few high-profile damages claims have reinforced this tendency, along with a wave of panic by insurance companies about the kinds of activities that youth workers used to do all the time (not always safely, mind you. I could tell you some stories…). A legitimate concern with risk assessment and management, in line with *Stevenson* and non-maleficence, has deteriorated into risk *avoidance*. The real issue is not the avoidance of harm to the young person, but harm to the agency or a worker if the young person sues.

This approach has bled into youth workers' own approaches. Youth work commentary on the *Every Child Matters* (Chief Secretary to the Treasury 2003) agenda includes statements like:

> Youth work can also help all young people explore issues of risk and develop their ability to recognise and practise behaviour that minimises their exposure to risk.
>
> (Tomsett and Groves 2006: 17; National Youth Agency nd)

I suspect the problem is in the wording rather than the intention. My criticism would be that youth workers aren't necessarily trying to minimise young people's exposure to risk. Exposure to *harm*, but not exposure to risk. Exposure to risk is a critical part of young people's development. Often, it is our job to increase risk.

There is a standard shopping list of risks for young people: drugs, crime, early pregnancy, unemployment, homelessness. These get a lot of media attention, but there is also a range of risks for young people that don't. Things like: the risk of passivity, of resignation; of cynicism; of lowered sights and stunted aspiration; of isolation; of premature foreclosure. Working with young people to combat the harms that result from these things will often involve taking risks. There are big risks in doing your first speech in front of a hall of people, or taking the microphone at a karaoke, or a lead role in a piece of theatre. Or even walking up to a group of people you don't know.

Even in those areas that the newspapers are interested in, such as drugs or crime, the youth work strategy may not be about decreasing risks. There may be a range of penalties from a young person's group should the young person choose to opt out of group activities, including crime. To stand in the face of those penalties may involve taking huge risks and the potential for real harm. Our job is to help the young person assess the risk and decide what they want to do. And then to manage risk as best they can: by careful preparation, working through all the possibilities, maximising margins for error, covering the down-side, building in an escape route or a safe house or a contingency fund. Perhaps, in the long run, it might reduce the harm for the young person. But perhaps not. It might just be about the way they want to live, about life being better, or being free. A better life is not always a safer one.

Helping young people manage risk

A standard way in which financial institutions manage risk is by requiring a guarantor: a person who is prepared to shoulder the risk of the borrower by taking on the debt if they default. A lot of youth workers' work is like that. In principle, we treat young people as capable, responsible, competent human beings, *even if we know, at this moment, that this has not been demonstrated.* In the process of treating them as adults, they become adult.

There are obvious risks in this approach. Young people might fail. Jobs might not get done, money might go missing, phone calls might not get made. Individuals might panic at what they have to do, and regress. Someone might lose their temper and smash everything in the place. We go guarantor for those kinds of possibilities. We manage the risk. Because we manage the risk, people with resources are prepared to give young people access to buildings, hire vehicles, sound equipment and musical instruments, residential camp sites, hotel accommodation. In doing so, we create the opportunity for young people to be adult, to be agents, to make decisions and control outcomes.

As it does for any guarantor, this puts *us* at risk. Careful assessment will determine what a reasonable 'stretch' is for a given young person, and we take responsibility if we get it wrong. As with all risk assessment, we prepare well, make sure we have the information, assess the contingencies, cover the downside, support the young person if they don't make the distance. It is also a reason why the understanding and support of management is so critical. A youth worker can be very isolated and the work very stressful if management has no understanding of the risks that they are taking with young people and would not support them if they did (see Chapter 21).

Conclusion

Risk is a key resource in our work with young people. It frames the logic of our intervention. For most young people, the teenage years involve change. The process of change creates a flux within which settled things become unstable, certainties become contingent. This is precisely the dynamic that makes young people available for learning and for transformation, to take up new, sometimes completely different and unexpected, ways of being. It can also mean losing their way. The massive majority of young people don't, or at least not for very long, but it can happen. Becoming more independent while experience has yet to teach its lessons also exposes young people to a riskier environment.

The fact that young people don't usually have much power also means they are exposed to greater risks – they simply don't have the resources to defend themselves against exploiters, whether they be sexual predators, tabloid newspapers or populist politicians. In our role as advocates, we try to defend young people from this kind of maleficence.

However, risk is not harm. It is not our job to simply decrease the risks for young people. Arguably, young people need risk to develop capacities for sound judgement (Sercombe and Paus 2009). It is about helping young people to recognise, assess, face and manage risk. This may involve introducing new risks into young people's lives.

At the same time, if we do that, we are responsible for the process. Youth workers and the young people under their care have been amazingly lucky in my experience. There is no doubt that many of us have exposed young people to risks where we haven't made good assessments, where contingencies haven't been thought through, and the downside hasn't been covered. Fortunately, amid the things that could go wrong, usually nothing very serious does, or at least nothing that we won't recover from. But in my own practice, that has too often been good luck rather than good management, and it isn't good enough. When young people enter into a youth work relationship with us, they entrust their own persons to us. We have therefore a clear duty: a duty of care, a duty to avoid the likelihood of harm.

On the other hand, you don't need a lot of skill to practise risk avoidance. But then you aren't doing youth work any more. Indeed, sometimes, harm will eventuate, no matter how good our assessment. Accidents do happen: nobody's fault, no ethical breach. If a young person is harmed because of our failure to adequately assess and manage the risk, that is our fault. But if a young person is harmed – stunted, passive, repressed, fearful, undeveloped – because of our own unwillingness to take risks, that is also our ethical responsibility. Youth workers need to be unusually skilled in risk assessment and management: skilled enough to be brave, to defend their work before risk-averse authorities, to take on risks for and with young people, and to work with young people through the risk.

14

PROFESSIONAL BOUNDARIES AND DUAL RELATIONSHIPS[1]

Summary

Youth workers, like other professionals, need to be clear about their boundaries, both in terms of the way that their professional relationship is constructed and the extension of the relationship with a young person into private time and space. The disciplining of these boundaries has sometimes been referred to as 'professional distance'. This chapter discusses whether distance is what this is about, or whether emotional connection is essential for youth work practice. The problems with dual relationships, where there is a multiplicity of roles, are also discussed.

The limited relationship

In Chapter 2, we described a professional relationship as intentionally limited. It is the limits of the relationship that define it, that create its quality, and that channel its energy. That is probably true of any relationship. What you will not do in a relationship is just as important as what you will. And different kinds of relationships (a marriage, for example, versus a friendship) have different codes for what you will and won't do. You need to know what your youth work relationship is about: what you are doing, and perhaps even more, what you are *not* doing. While our relationships with young people are open, friendly and respectful, and young people feel treated as an equal, there are some kinds of activities, some kinds of partnership, even some kinds of conversation that we won't get into with young people. This is especially true of interactions that entertain sexual possibilities, as we discussed in Chapter 12.

However, that isn't the only set of boundaries or limitations in the relationship, and there are characteristics of youth work as a profession which sometimes make the boundaries difficult to specify, and sometimes difficult for young people to recognise. The informal nature of youth work means that there often isn't a

[1] This chapter is based on an article published by the Australian Clearinghouse for Youth Studies: H. Sercombe (2009) 'Embedded youth work: Ethical questions for youth work professionals', in R. White (ed.), *Concepts and Methods of Youth Work*. Hobart: ACYS Publishing (reprinted from *Youth Studies Australia*, 2007, 26(2): 11–19). A version also appears in the second edition of Sarah Banks (2009) *Ethical Issues in Youth Work*. London: Routledge.

space or time boundary around the action: it isn't a 50-minute consultation in a counselling room with the door closed. The youth work relationship can feel like a friendship, with lots of the elements of friendship, such as good-natured ribbing and play. Language codes are often those that the young people use, so it can feel to them and to you like you are one of the gang.

In such a context, youth workers need to be clear about the nature of their relationship, and especially the limits of the relationship.

This relates both to *roles* – what kind of relationship template (e.g. friend, mother, confidante, teacher, peer-group leader) is projected and reproduced in the relationship – and *domains* – what will be the limits in different aspects of the relationship (such as time, space, money, emotion, availability). These interconnect, so that certain role templates will project certain domain boundaries and expectations. For example, friends are generally available to each other in leisure time. Professionals and clients are not available to each other in leisure time. Family creates obligations regardless of affinity (i.e. whether you like them), friendship doesn't.

Role approximations

The difficulty can be that a young person may never have met a youth worker before, so will have to work hard to make sense of the relationship. In order for this to happen, the youth worker needs to be crystal clear about the nature of youth work practice. If the youth worker is messy in their conception of the relationship, you can expect the young person to be too.

The standard way people work out how to behave in a new kind of relationship is to approximate the new relationship to an existing template. Often, that is to see us as a kind of teacher or social worker. However, it will be quickly apparent to young people that you aren't one of those because the relationship will (and should) feel different. Young people regularly report that the youth work relationship is where they feel treated as an equal (Merton et al. 2004; Spence and Devanney 2006). The closest template to this is often that of a friend.

A friend?

This role approximation can be appealing both to young people and to youth workers. However, it is not accurate, and is misleading sometimes to the point of being dangerous. If, for example, you count the young people you work with as friends, and they see you in the same way, what are the rules? Do you drop in at their house and hang out? Do they come round to yours? Do you invite them to your parties? Do you go to the movies together, other than as a youth service activity? Do you go to the pub together? If you do, do you buy each other alcohol? There is also the fact that we are generally paid or otherwise mandated to be there. There is something a bit wrong about being paid to be someone's friend.

As a generalisation, you are not your clients' friend. You are their youth worker. It is no less a warm and caring relationship, but there are obligations and responsibilities you have as their youth worker that you do not have as their friend, and vice versa. Your answer to a young person saying 'But I thought you were my friend!' should always be clear and unequivocal. That was never what it was about. You were never their friend: you are their youth worker.

A second mum?

Another template for some workers is that of 'mum' (for some reason, the 'dad' approximation doesn't seem so common). This is an appealing, caring and nurturing role, and many of the young people that we work with may not have great relationships with their own mums. It is easy for workers to be drawn into surrogate motherhood as a template for the relationship.

Mother-roles in a youth work context are not, in themselves, a bad thing. Many traditional societies actively organise multiple mothers within the culture, in recognition of this need. It is fine to have mum-type workers as volunteers in youth agencies, and 'camp mum and dad' is a standard and rich tradition in residential or camping contexts. But it is important to be careful in both the naming and explanation of such roles. They aren't youth workers. If they are youth workers, don't call them mum and dad.

Some youth accommodation services have worked with role descriptions of workers as 'house parents' or similar designations. Again, there isn't anything wrong with that, and the way that many care agencies are set up evoke short-term foster family models. But, the limitations and boundaries of these relationships need to be clear, including the way that they differ from real parents. This doesn't necessarily need to be explained in explicit detail to young people, except when boundaries are being crossed or there are boundary mistakes being made. Generally, if the youth worker is clear, is acting consistently within their role, and corrects boundary crossings when they occur, young people will work out pretty quickly how to find the complementary role.

Dual relationships

Things can also get difficult in situations where you have a relationship with a young person in a youth work setting, but also know them in some other setting. They may work at your hairdressers, or go to your church, for instance. Or you might routinely end up at the same nightclub. In this situation, the roles and rules can easily become confused (Gottlieb 1993), and the boundaries start to shift and become uncertain. The sites where this can emerge are expanding all the time with the advent of social networking sites and the possibility of out-of-work 'friend' type contacts online.

This is a bit of an occupational hazard if you are part of the community in which you are working, and have multiple loyalties and obligations because of this. For example:

* **Work in small towns.** You can't avoid multiple relationships there because there are more roles than people and everyone is doing a range of things. And there isn't any choice. In the city, you can choose to go to a different pub from the one your clients drink at. Or get your plumbing fixed by someone other than your client's dad. (Younggren 2003; Sercombe 2006).

- **Work in ethnic or cultural communities**. Communities of difference, such as the LGBT (lesbian, gay, bisexual or transgender) community, may have similar characteristics (Schank and Skovholt 1997).
- **Work with family-based communities**. Aboriginal, Maori or Traveller communities, for example. Traditional communities are often made up of people who are related in some way, either by blood or marriage. It is the relationship that makes you part of the community (if you don't have a family connection, the community may even invent one for you).
- **Situations where young people are living with you in your home**. In general, this is frowned on in youth work circles, but there is no clear consensus about it. You are then a parent-figure, a house-mate, or a landlord or landlady, as well as their youth worker. This can also be the case in youth accommodation programmes.
- **Situations where young people who are clients of a service are promoted to work as volunteers within the service and perhaps then as paid staff**. Their peer group, established while they were a client of the service, may still be very much engaged, so their peers are now their clients.

Across a number of different professions, this has generally been referred to as the *dual relationships problem* (see Corey et al. 2007; Sercombe 2010). In the literature on ethics in professions such as law, medicine and psychology, there have been extensive debates around this problem. The general consensus is that you should avoid dual relationships wherever you can because it is difficult to avoid conflicts of interest, that is, what you should be doing in one role conflicts with what you should be doing in the other (Corey et al. 2007). Special care needs to be taken to preserve the integrity of the youth work relationship, and to defend it against the confusion of multiple roles.

Example

Suppose you know, in your role as a youth worker, that your nephew is using drugs. You also know that your sister, his mum, doesn't know. Are you going to tell? If you don't, and something bad happens to him and it comes out that you knew that he was using, how is your sister going to feel about that? How is your reputation going to be in your family? Your obligation as a youth worker is clear: you keep confidences. The information belongs to the young person, and it isn't yours to hand around. Your obligation as an aunt or uncle and a sister or brother to his mum is also pretty clear: you should probably pass on information that they need in order to care for their son effectively, especially if he is at immediate risk.

In this instance, the two sets of obligations directly contradict each other. And if your nephew tells you something as his youth worker, he has an absolute right to expect that confidence to be kept, and to feel betrayed if you were to break that confidence and tell his mum. And if some damage occurred to him because you broke confidence (e.g. his mum threw him out), he would be well within his rights to sue for professional malpractice.

Avoiding dual-role problems or managing them

The consensus across the professions is that dual relationships are to be avoided if at all possible (Corey et al. 2007). So, as a youth worker, if you happen to run across a client at the pub, you smile and say hi and turn back to your own group of friends. You don't join them and buy them a drink and kick on to the nightclub with them when the pub closes. If you don't have any friends other than the young people, you need help.

Some principles for practice

If the dual relationship can't be avoided, strategies must be put in place to keep the relationships separate and the separate roles clear, distinct and quarantined from each other. Here are some suggestions (we called them policies) which we developed for the guidance of our workers in one community. They might help.

- Be clear about your role – about who and what you are as a youth worker. Reflect on what your obligations are under your professional role and in your other role (Schank and Skovholt 1997). In this way you can identify where potential conflicts might arise.
- Be open and transparent with your peers about the potential for role conflict (Gottlieb 1993). In this way, we can hold each other accountable and catch role conflict short when it happens. Having a colleague who is also watching helps. In every case of role conflict, your supervisor ought to be notified of the potential for conflict of interest. This is yet another situation where routine professional supervision is important. And if you are reluctant to tell your supervisor, it may be a sign that something is dodgy.
- Wherever possible, do not work with the client alone. Teamwork can dilute and offset dangers that exist in role confusion, and can help keep you in your youth worker role and accountable to that role.
- Communicate clearly with the young person and with other stakeholders about the dual role and what your different roles require of you. If your sister in the above example knows that you cannot pass on information about your nephew that you have gained in the youth work relationship, no matter what the circumstances (short of the normal limits to confidentiality),

(Continued)

(Continued)

and you can all endorse that stance, then harm might be avoided if and when an actual situation arises. And your client, the nephew, knows what he can trust you with and what he can't.

- If role conflict is common or unavoidable within your field of practice, as it is in small towns, in situations where the practice is to promote clients into professional roles, and in relationship-defined communities such as Aboriginal communities, codes of practice ought to be written into policy and procedures manuals so that everyone is clear about the game and practitioners aren't always having to work it out individually. Training and professional development is critical in these settings.

The onus of responsibility for the consequences of dual relationships, according to Corey, Corey and Callanan (2007), rests with the professional. If you enter into a dual relationship, it is up to you, not the young person, to manage the complexities involved.

Some people are good at quarantining different roles, at compartmentalising different kinds of relationships in their heads. Some aren't. If you cannot maintain a clear and distinct professional role with a young person because of a dual relationships problem, you might need to withdraw from that relationship and facilitate support for the young person with someone else. If dual relationships are endemic in the situation in which you work, you might need another job.

Domain limitations

Alongside role boundaries, and often connected strongly to them, the professional relationship also involves limitations in the kind of domain that the relationship will enter into, and the extent to which the relationship is allowed to enter into that domain. For example, the professional relationship is a relationship in the public world. The extent to which young people are given access to our private worlds will be limited. As we suggested above, we wouldn't generally invite young people to our parties or to go out socially. Unlike parents, the kind of time and the amount of time we would spend with a young person will also be limited.

A clear consensus on what these limitations are has not been established within the youth work field, and I'm not sure that it should be. The contexts and communities within which youth workers and young people live vary enormously, and what would be too personal in one setting would be too restrictive in another. But understanding our role means that we aren't open to all offers or all demands, and the point is to be clear about the role so that clarity about these things follows. *You need to have boundaries and to know what they are.* Again, this may change with context, role and the nature of the community in which you work.

If there is a general rule, it is that commercial relationships with young people are a bad idea, buying and selling goods in particular. Whatever the advantages to both parties, the practice of selling goods to young people or buying from them is fraught with risks about the origin of the goods, disputes over payment, second thoughts about the fairness of the price, faulty goods or dissatisfaction with them – all of which could jeopardise the youth work relationship, which is what you are there for. You wreck that and it could mean that a young person now does not have access to a youth work service, because you have not protected the youth work relationship. Don't do it.

Domain boundaries to consider

Time

- What is your position on young people contacting you out of hours? Do you respond or refer them to a crisis care agency with a 24-hour mandate?
- What do you do if a young person knocks on your door in the middle of the night?
- Do you have concerns if a young person wants to spend all their free time with you?
- Do young people have your personal mobile phone number?

Money

- Do you lend money to young people? What do you do about following up repayment?

How much access to your private life?

- Do young people have your home phone number? Do they know where you live and do they drop in for a chat?
- If they do, are they welcome? Do you invite them in or chat at the door?
- Would you invite them to stay for dinner if it was dinner time?

Transport

- Would you give a young person a lift in your car? How far out of your way would you go?

Personal space

- What is your position on physical contact with young people you work with, including touching, hugging, horseplay or contact sports?

The concept of professional distance

One of the ways that domain limitations are sometimes talked about is through the concept of professional distance (National Youth Agency 2002). This can refer to any of the domains mentioned in this chapter, but especially the degree of emotional connection or investment made in the relationship. You will hear workers talking about people becoming 'too emotionally involved', for example. Sometimes, this kind of concept is extended into notions of 'professional objectivity' or 'neutrality' (Ministry for Youth Development 2001).

In some professions, this way of understanding emotional boundaries makes sense. A surgeon, perhaps, needs to disregard the emotional life of the patient as he or she cuts the patient open. Lawyers need a fine appreciation for the logic of the narrative and which arguments will work in court, independently of a client's outrage or feeling of injustice. Engineers need to put aside the wishful thinking of clients in making design recommendations.

Youth work is not like that. The kind of transformation that we are interested in involves the emotions: it is to no small extent a transformation in the emotions themselves. Our capacity for empathy, to be able to connect with the emotional state of the young person we are working with, to understand the emotional space and to work with a young person in it – these are core skills of youth workers. You can't do it if you are not emotionally available.

Neither are we neutral or objective. We are advocates for the young people we work with, and work primarily to see things from their perspective, though we would always want to understand as many different points of view as we can. But we are biased in favour of young people: this is an ethical choice.

There are emotional disciplines that youth workers need to exercise. Young people's disclosures can often be shocking, and a worker's immediate emotional reactions can spill over in ways that aren't helpful. For a variety of reasons, a worker's emotional reactions can be disproportionate, for example, a worker's grief reaction at hearing of a young person's loss may be bigger than the young person's. Or, in a crisis, we can be immobilised by our emotional reactions when young people need us to be cool and decisive and just to get things sorted. In positions where there is high emotional traffic, we may also need to discipline our emotional engagement so that we are not emotionally exhausted and burnt out (see Chapter 21).

Sometimes, our emotional state can be more about ourselves, our own histories, about unresolved conflicts or losses or disappointments in our own lives. Emotional expressiveness can be indulgent, and some people enjoy the drama of emotional connectedness with a young person. Then, the intervention is no longer about the young person, but about us.

We may also have emotional reactions against the things young people say and do. This again needs to be disciplined. Young people may express opinions and lifestyles of which we disapprove, but our task is to work with young people on these things. Giving full rein to our emotional reactions may prevent effective intervention rather than facilitating it.

This discipline is not about 'distance'. A youth worker may be the 'closest' person in a young person's life. The youth work relationship is often deeply emotionally engaged; the youth worker is emotionally present. It isn't unprofessional to love the young people you work with. On the contrary, it is precisely this kind of connection that can open up possibilities for life to be different. However, this real, authentic emotional reaction to young people happens within the context of a youth work relationship, and is shaped and disciplined by that relationship.

Conclusion

There are good reasons why the professional tradition, with its understanding of the professional relationship as limited and privileged, has such a significant influence in practices which involve the proper and safe care of vulnerable people. Care about the limits of the professional role and care about the reach of the relationship into various domains of our lives protects the relationship, and avoids conflicts and complications that might compromise it.

The actual expression of these limits will vary from context to context, agency to agency, community to community. For example, complete avoidance of dual relationships might be impossible, and the maintenance of integrity in the face of multiple relationships can be hard. I have been involved in dual relationships myself, both as a client and as a professional, sometimes by necessity, sometimes by choice. Sometimes they have worked well, and we have been able to preserve both roles, and even to enrich them. Sometimes that hasn't happened, and one role has contaminated the other to the detriment of both.

The need to be clear and careful is especially relevant for youth workers because our way of working tends to promote relationships in which the power differences are kept in the background, the communication style feels like a friendship, and the professional encounter is not neatly circumscribed in time and space. Under these circumstances, awareness, debate, guidance and the pursuit of clarity about good practice is essential for the safety and integrity both of youth workers and young people.

15

THE ETHICS OF POWER[1]

Summary

This chapter tries to clarify some of the fundamental questions involved in the ethics of power. Namely, what is power? What are the proper conditions for its use? And what ethical considerations arise from our understanding of these things? Rather than attempt to cover a range of perspectives, the chapter presents a theory of power developed from a contractarian perspective, that is, that understanding human relationships (including ethics) as based on a kind of contract or agreement, whether overt or implied, makes the terms of power relationships open and accountable.

Power is perhaps the largest single dynamic in the emergence of ethical questions: many ethical concepts that are central to youth work practice, such as 'oppression', 'corruption' and 'injustice', rely on an understanding of power to make sense. It is power, for example, that determines who gets to be just (or unjust) to whom. A lot of the work on theories of power has been developed within the disciplines of political philosophy, politics and sociology, rather than in moral philosophy. An ethics is often implicit within the conceptions of power developed in these fields. For example, there is an ethics of power implicit within Marx's social theory, within feminism, within fascist thought and in liberal democratic theory. When they argue about where power *does* come from, there is always an agenda operating about where it *should* come from. In many of these accounts, it is the dark side of power that is being explored: the practice of power that results in injustice, inequality and oppression.

For some commentators, and for some youth workers, all relations which involve power differentials are, by definition, oppressive and unjust. I don't think this helps us very much, though. Social life inevitably generates power

---

[1] This chapter is based on an article published by the Australian Clearinghouse for Youth Studies: H. Sercombe, (2009) 'Embedded youth work: Ethical questions for youth work professionals', in R. White (ed.), *Concepts and Methods of Youth Work*. Hobart: ACYS Publishing (reprinted from H. Sercombe (1998) 'Power, ethics and youth work', *Youth Studies Australia,* 17(1): 18–23).

differentials, whether recognised or not. Any division of labour will move power towards some people and away from others. There are no communities *without* power processes, at least at the informal level of popularity, influence and differential respect. Wherever a relationship is mobilised for some kind of joint action, you have a power relation. It seems to me to be better to recognise not only the inevitability but the *productiveness* of the exercise of power (Foucault 1984), and to work out how it should operate ethically. We cripple ourselves if we don't understand it.

So, because youth work is a relationship, it is a power relationship. Youth workers have sometimes claimed that the relationship with young people is an 'equal' relationship. This is, I think, disingenuous and also dangerous. If we are not aware of the nature of the power that we have, it becomes hard to avoid the corruptions to which any exercise of power is susceptible. If we are to understand our own practice, we need a clear understanding of the basis and practice of our power. As such, the classical ethical notions of legitimacy, of consent, of force, of authority, and of coercion, become important.

This is not to say, of course, that youth workers always have the power in a youth work setting, or in all the processes that happen in a youth work setting. Management can determine or constrain what goes on. There are always shifting alliances between youth workers and key powerful young people, and young people can either allow or not allow youth work to happen in a setting. Part of standard youth work practice is also to relinquish power, to enable the exercise of power by young people even when the youth worker has formal and institutional authority.

Recent thinking in the theory of power

Over the last few years, postmodernist and poststructuralist theory has turned its attention to the question of power, not at the level of the formal structures of the state, or of other clearly defined social institutions with formally constituted processes of power and domination, but to the level of the informal processes of everyday life – the family, shopping, the parking inspector, sitting in classrooms – and, by implication, youth work. For Foucault especially:

> power comes from below ... there is no binary and all-encompassing opposition between rulers and ruled at the root of power relations, and serving as a general matrix. ... One must suppose rather that the manifold relations of force that take shape and come into play in the machinery of production, in families, in limited groups and institutions, are the basis for wide-ranging effects of cleavage that run through the social body as a whole.
>
> (Foucault 1984: 94)

For Foucault and others, power becomes diffused throughout the whole network of social relationships, with every relation a source of processes of domination and subordination, established and confirmed in the construction of discourse, of language. Power has no centre. It flourishes and reproduces itself in the patterns of the most ordinary interactions between people, the most taken-for-granted conversations, the shape of buildings and the layout of rooms, the conventions about who sits where at the dinner table. And, of course, in groups of young people, in youth centres, in relations between youth workers and young people.

This is an interesting idea. The move away from a concept of power as belonging to individuals or institutions, as constituted in rules and laws, as originating at the top and being diffused through to the bottom, and where one party 'has' the power and another 'has not', makes a real difference to our understanding. The notion of power as constituted in *relationships*, rather than institutions, sends us off to look for the exercise of power in rather interesting places.

There are some limitations in Foucault's approach. He doesn't define power, for one thing. He mostly deals with the analysis and description of its processes. In the seminal passages in *The History of Sexuality* (1984), Foucault just uses a synonym, 'force relations'. Beyond this, he describes the *techniques* and *operations* of power with great insight, but does not look for a definition of power itself. Let's see if we can take that forward a little.

Power as a mutual relationship

Foucault argues that power is not something that the big guys 'have', to be exercised over the little guys. The subordinate do not merely and passively obey. There is a complex mutual relation in play, in which the subordinate are as active in constructing the power relation as the dominant. *A practice of domination must be answered by a practice of subordination.* The existence of rule depends on compliance. The subordinate *cooperate* with the dominant in a power system, though often not quite as the dominant would like. Logically, the ruled could withdraw their cooperation and the rulers would no longer be rulers. The structure of power would collapse.

In this idea, the standard understanding of who 'allows' and who 'is allowed' to act is turned on its head. The ruled *allow* the rulers to act in certain ways by continuing to comply. If they were to withhold their compliance, the ruler would be unable to act. It is important to think through the mechanism by which this power relation is constituted.

One approach is the idea of *mandate*. In this understanding, at its simplest, the relation of power involves one party (me, say) *ceding* (giving up, handing over) to another (you, say) the *mandate* to act on his/her behalf. As such, it involves me being prepared to comply or cooperate with your actions, exercised, as they were, in my name. *This relation of cession is the primary power relation.* I allow you to manage my accounts, to represent me on the committee, to work on my car. As such, by handing over my power to act on these matters to you, I subject myself to you – to your judgements, your priorities. Within the limited scope of the matter in question, I give you my power. The amount of power you get is a function of the number of matters over which I give you a mandate, and how strategic these matters are.

In the social context, this relation is multiplied. Collective action is stronger than individual action. When more than two people are involved, the agreement to cede power is often made cooperatively. Together, we allow someone (Rex, say) to act on behalf of all of us.

It can be easily seen that such an agreement is more weighty than an agreement between me and you. If five of us agree together to give Rex a mandate to manage our finances, say, then Rex wields the collective force of five of us, rather than just one. I may decide that I want to withdraw from the agreement, and no longer put my money in the fund or take any responsibility for what happens with the fund. But in doing so, I face Rex, and behind him, four other people. If my action is not supported, I face them alone, and may face other penalties rather than merely the loss of the advantages of cooperative financing. They may decide they don't want to be my friend any more, for example. The amount of power Rex gets is a function of the number of subjects who cede him a mandate. In this view, then:

> Power is a relation in which one party cedes to another the mandate to act on their behalf.
>
> We could call the people who cede (or hand over, or give up, or relinquish) their power a *constituency*, and the person(s) to whom a mandate is given a *delegate*.

A number of things follow from this sort of explanation. First, power relations are not necessarily evil or destructive, but are usually necessary for cooperative living or cooperative action. Even the simplest level of cooperative action, such as the division of labour, involves a devolution of power.

Second, most of the power relations that I am involved in have never been the subject of a conscious choice. Many of them were relations that I was born into. Most of them are, indeed, invisible to me – or rather, I am blind and deaf to them. It is only when I become aware of them that I am placed in a position of choice. This does not alter the fact that they are still power relations in which I actively participate whether as dominant or subordinate, whether as authority or subject.

Third, no person is powerless. Each person has at least the power of action that a human being has, and can cede or not cede their power to some other. At any point, a person may withdraw the mandate given to others to act on their behalf, whether that power has been handed over willingly or unwillingly. It may be that the other person may indeed carry out whatever threat or damage, even to the point of death, but a mandate cannot be taken or stolen. It must be given, it must be ceded. I may be drugged, restrained, imprisoned so that I cannot carry out my will to (for example) leave or speak, but I cannot be required to stay or remain silent. Think about Socrates or

Jesus or Nelson Mandela or Mahatma Gandhi. I can be immobilised, but I cannot be deprived of my own power. Each person has the power of at least one human being.

Fourth, a given individual may wield many times the power of one human being within a given sphere, or *scope*, of activity. The head of state of a large country may wield the power of many millions of people in a rather broader but not limitless scope of activity. The amount of power an individual has is a function of the number of people who have ceded power and the range of spheres of activity over which a mandate has been ceded. It is difficult, as a person with a small constituency or even only the power of one, to face a person with a large constituency and scope, and the collateral penalties involved in such a confrontation can be severe.

Fifth, there is such a thing as *perceived power* here. A delegate may have a small constituency and scope, or even no constituency at all, but if I believe that they do, I may well defer to them.

Sixth, it is not necessary to the power relation that a mandate be ceded willingly or voluntarily. Rex may have blackmailed me, or he may have threatened to bash me if I did not vote for him. Under the circumstances, it might be prudent for me to cede, but it is still me who cedes. All that is required for the power relation to exist is that I cede. It is a *de facto* thing. If I allow a situation to exist and continue, I maintain the power relation, and will do so until I actively withdraw my mandate. I do not even have to be aware that the power relation exists, that I have ceded anything, that I had anything to cede. Rex's family might have always managed the finances for my family, and it might never occur to me that it could be otherwise. There might be all sorts of stories that we tell which imply that their managing the finances is natural and non-negotiable. Nevertheless, as long as I comply, as long as my money stays in the fund, I cede my power.

Seventh, structures of power (such as hierarchy) work to aggregate the constituency and scope of activity, and to 'naturalise' and stabilise the cession of power. Force or threats of force can be used to achieve compliance, but it is an expensive tool because it makes the exercise of power continuously visible. Measures which construct consent, or hide the power relationship from view, are much more economical.

Ethical considerations

There are a number of ethical considerations for youth workers which might be usefully clarified by this approach. A relation is **coercive** when a penalty is threatened or implied for not entering into a contract, where compliance has been gained through 'force or fraud', rather than given willingly. A power relation is **legitimate** where power has been ceded voluntarily and without coercion. Of course, a person might agree to the imposition of a penalty if they break the contract, but as long as the *agreement* is unforced, that would still be legitimate.

Corruption is when a person uses the power given by a constituency to further their own interests *to the detriment of the interests of their constituency*. For example, when a youth worker advances themselves at the expense of young people. We'll talk about that more in Chapter 17.

Oppression means that someone uses the power ceded by a constituency *against* the constituency. So when police, vested with the power to use force to uphold the law, use the instruments of force in contravention of the law, or against people who are law-abiding, that is oppression.

Dependency becomes a problem when the worker takes on too wide a scope of activity (among other things, see Chapter 16). If the client wishes to withdraw, the costs may be too high. I might not like the accommodation a youth housing service provides, but if I leave, will I also lose my income, my only close human contact, my major source of information and guidance, my chief means of transport, my key to other networks and other resources?

Empowerment, on the other hand, refers to the process of a constituent becoming active in the power relation, becoming aware of the power relations that they are involved in, aware of their duties as a constituent and of the duties of their delegates (see Chapter 16), and holding their delegates accountable for the power they have been given.

Conclusion

The youth work relationship is a power relationship. Young people give us their power to act on their behalf. It is really important, then, for us to be clear about who the constituency is, what the ambit of the mandate is, what mutual obligations flow from the relationship. The power that workers exercise over and on behalf of young people is a legitimate consequence of a clear and informed mandate, not something gained through personal charm or kindness, the boundaries of which are ill-defined or invisible and subject to corruption. It is not necessary that we like each other, though it is, of course, a nice thing. Trust is important, as it is in any contracting situation, but there should also be clear avenues for redress if the mandate is not being fulfilled, or if the relationship is becoming corrupt or oppressive. Young people should be trained to exercise these options.

This brings us back to the idea of the young person as the primary client. Youth workers operate under multiple contracts with multiple constituencies. In any given incident, the interests of a whole range of constituencies may be tapping us on the shoulder, demanding that their mandate be fulfilled. Routinely, these will include management committees, other professionals, funding bodies, peers, the broader community, parents and others, the broader group of young people as well as the young person concerned. Many of these demands may be contradictory. Youth work as a practice gives a priority to the mandate established by young people as the primary constituency. As we discussed in Chapters 8 and 9, funding is accepted from governments, churches and other bodies on the understanding that it will be used to operationalise this mandate, given the lack of resources available to young people to exercise on their own behalf and to pay for the advocacy that they need. Management, if it is to manage *youth work*, exists under the same mandate, derived from the same constituency.

The following chapters will try to work through the ethics of this in practice, as youth workers try to struggle with their own interests versus the interests of young people, the process of and limits to empowerment, and youth work interventions in the broader political environment.

16

EMPOWERMENT AND DEPENDENCY IN THE YOUTH WORK RELATIONSHIP

Summary

Youth workers often work in situations of great need, where young people feel deeply powerless over anything much in their lives. Working with young people to develop their sense of agency, of being able to make decisions and be active in their own lives and their own futures, is at the core of the purpose of youth work. Yet the dynamic of intervention can often generate patterns of relationship in which young people are dependent on youth workers for the satisfaction of a wide range of needs. This chapter explores this, and offers suggestions for avoiding the ethical traps that can emerge while still offering young people the right amount of support.

The language of empowerment has had a pervasive presence in youth work discourse since the 1980s. Its actual origins are obscure. According to Batliwala (2007), the term seems to have emerged from the swirl of social action and liberation movements of the 1970s, and quickly gained currency across a wide range of development and social intervention domains. Because of its availability to describe both political and personal, collective and individual processes, it was also quickly co-opted by mainstream liberal, self-help and business interests. By the 1990s the term had become fashionable, a 'buzzword', and because it meant all things to all people, its meaning became diluted (Batliwala 2007). Critical, collective and oppositional elements of the word became sidelined or edited out, and it became a kind of synonym for 'self-actualisation'. By 2005, Tony Jeffs reports that 'in the 1970s we had enfranchisement; 1980s participation; 1990s empowerment; and now citizenship'. Empowerment, like these other terms, was 'just another "spray-on word"' (Jeffs 2005: 1).

However, while the term was rarely well defined or articulated, it had an immediate affective impact in most youth work contexts. At its peak, it was taken by many practitioners to express the core of what youth work was about, and for many, it still does. The latest version of competences for Community Learning and Development in Scotland, which embraces youth work, identifies empowerment as a core value (Standards Council for Community Learning and

Development 2009). In 2005, the Commonwealth Youth Programme placed empowerment at the centre of its strategic plan and the core of its defining statements (Commonwealth Youth Programme 2005). The Youth Affairs Council of Australia's 1983 landmark document *Creating Tomorrow Today* established empowerment as *the* defining concept for youth work (Youth Affairs Council of Australia 1983). In Britain, the Second Ministerial Conference of 1991 said that:

> Youth work is about empowerment – supporting young people to increase their confidence in expressing themselves, their needs, their desires, the fulfilments. It's about them being able to communicate with other people and make constructive decisions while taking into account the different options available and the possible consequences.
>
> [This] starts where young people are at, is dictated by their needs, goes at their pace, and is flexible to fit different situations. Even though this may look casual to the outsider, or even to the young people, it represents very deliberate interventions by the youth worker.
>
> (Young 2006)

As a buzzword, empowerment is probably now past its prime. The National Youth Agency has removed it from its defining statements, for example (Banks 1999). However, we are here concerned with the ethical content of words like this, not just how fashionable they are. If the word once meant something, it may still do, and, paradoxically, empowerment's slide from the A-list might give us the opportunity to have another look at the concept without the hype, and to explore the ethical issues that the concept seeks to name. As Batliwala suggests, it may be due for rehabilitation.

Empowerment and ethics

If the documents cited above represent accurately the purpose of youth work, empowerment is not optional, not one among many possible approaches to working with young people. *Youth work that does not empower young people is unethical*. In this, the codes of ethics agree.

In Chapter 3, we discussed the aims of youth work in terms of the key transformation that youth workers are looking for in their work with young people. This was described as facilitating the ethical agency of young people, in which they are able to see their lives as something belonging to them, in which they can actually decide how they are going to be, rather than be passive recipients, even victims, of a life determined by others or prescribed by circumstance. They take responsibility for those decisions, and take their place in the world as active, competent, full participants.

We know that the capacity of young people to take responsibility varies. This is the logic of preventing young people taking on certain responsibilities until a certain age. However, if you wait until someone has demonstrated responsibility before you give them any, they never develop those capacities. As we argued in

Chapter 13, facilitating ethical agency means giving young people responsibility before they have demonstrated the capacity to use it. As Vygotsky argued (Vygotsky 1962, 1978), that is the way you learn: by doing things you don't know how to do, under the watchful eye of someone who does.

If our standard practice is about helping young people learn how to be adult, to be agents in their own lives, the way we work is to invite young people to be adult even though they aren't one yet. We give them access to tasks and responsibilities which we know they are not at this point capable of executing, and then walk alongside them while they stretch out to meet the responsibility that we have offered. Youth workers look for that glimmer of potential that indicates a young person could stretch out to chair a meeting, scale a wall, talk to a stranger, challenge a local councillor, travel to a foreign country, confront their abuser. They set up activities or programmes that 'scaffold' the experience – that support it and make it safe to try. If the young person doesn't succeed, they support them in the recovery and in their next attempt. Part of the great skill of youth workers is being able to see these possibilities in young people, and to generate experiences that will make the potential real. And for young people to see that we can see these possibilities in them. This is at the core of youth work practice: it is how youth work normally operates.

Whether 'empowerment' as a term to describe this quality of agency will survive isn't clear. There are good reasons why names for it seem to have such a short half-life. Agency is a necessary and valuable quality for any society: we need people to take responsibility, to be active. However, it is a two-edged sword. People who are agents are not necessarily compliant, and tend to be more active in making power-holders accountable. The authorities would like people to be active citizens, but on their terms – to still be compliant, obedient, not to cause trouble. Unfortunately, you don't get one without the other. So authorities typically try to foster agency and sabotage it at the same time. Promoting a discourse (such as the empowerment discourse) and then dismantling it is one way to do this.

What empowerment does *not* mean

- Empowerment does not mean giving someone more power. A young person may already have plenty and may be abusing it. And someone may have lots of power (e.g. a young person who is wealthy) but not be empowered in the sense of living actively and taking responsibility for the life they have.
- Empowerment does not mean that we 'give' power to young people. As Jeffs and Smith argue: 'We don't change people, people change themselves in interaction with others. To talk of empowering people is thus to risk being anti-liberatory. ... Power is a feature of relationships. It is not something to be given or gifted' (2005: 21).

(Continued)

(Continued)

- Empowerment does not mean a person doing everything for themselves. The ultra-wealthy do almost nothing for themselves. They have other people do it for them. What they do, however, is hold those people accountable for the mandate they give them.
- It does not mean the withdrawal of essential supports, on budgetary grounds, in order to force people to be more self-sufficient (Crimmens and Whalen 1999).

Dependency

Alongside the virtue of empowerment often lies the vice of dependency (Harrison and Wise 2005). Paradoxically, dependency can be the product of a process of enabling or empowerment. Empowerment often involves assisting a person to leave an oppressive environment or situation or way of living. For example, a young person is helped to leave a violent household by finding a place in a youth refuge, or break out of heavy drug dependence. Initially, however, because the environment or lifestyle they left may be the only one they know, they might rely heavily on the person who enabled them to leave until they learn how to live with their new circumstances.

Oppressive situations can also be heavily conditioning. The young person might be used to not being able to make decisions or initiate action. It can be very painful having to learn, and the young person may be very keen for this nice new person in their life to make all their decisions for them. Sometimes, young people can be very skilled in getting a youth worker to accept this kind of mandate by playing on their protective instinct, telling them that they are the only person they can trust, or the only person they can talk to, or by overemphasising how fragile they are and how easily they could be forced to return to their old life. Indeed, this skill may have been critical to their earlier survival.

This kind of endorsement can be very affirming, even addictive, for a worker. Being able to establish rapport and trust with young people who may have a history of disengagement or maltreatment is a great skill and an affirmation of character as well as the core professional quality for good youth work. If youth workers are not secure professionally, or aren't clear about who they are and what they are doing, this can be the evidence they need to feel good about themselves – indeed, to feel empowered. The process of transference which we talked about in Chapter 12, can also be at play here. Transference is when a young person credits the youth worker with all the positive change in their life (or damns them for all the negative things that are happening in their life, or for things not working) even though it may be substantially a result of their own hard work or just something that was ready to happen. Youth workers can find themselves playing for that transference, working to create situations in which young people see them as wonderful. At its most pathological, youth workers can actually provoke crises, consciously or unconsciously, or sabotage young peoples' moves towards stability, because they need to be able to gallop in on the white horse and rescue.

Power can be corrupting, including the power that young people give us (see Chapter 17). The more power in play, the more likely it is to be corrupting, and the more likely we are to meet our own needs and our own interests at the expense of the young person. A young person in a dependent relationship with a youth worker is giving them a wide mandate, a lot of power. The first rule of politics (one of the many) is that people with power don't easily give it up. It takes discipline for us to construct youth work relationships in which the young person always has responsibility for the power they give to us, and can take it back at any time. Sometimes, as Rousseau (1762/2006) argued, people need to be 'forced to be free', and young people may need us to be insistent that they take their own power back.

Cues for avoiding dependency

- Recognise where you are offering support, and what would need to happen for the support to be taken up by others or taken back by young people themselves.
- Don't accept a mandate where 'you are the only person I can talk to'. The young person needs to learn to talk to other people too. How can you help organise that?
- Be cautious about situations with young people where you feel flattered. Especially if young people think you are 'wonderful'. You aren't, not very often anyway. Learn to recognise transference.
- Be suspicious of constant crisis, either in your own practice or the practice of your agency or colleagues.
- Spread the professional load. Facilitate the young person building a relationship with other workers.
- Refer. Don't take too wide a mandate. Use other professionals around you.
- Help the young person build a 'normal' support base: a mix of friends, family, fellow students or co-workers, and professional support.

Necessary dependency?

Having said that, dependency might be necessary when a young person is in crisis. A young person may not know what to do, and be in no psychological condition to do it even if they did. A person might be beside themselves with grief or pain, and there may be intensive emotional support needed. Sometimes, as a youth worker, you just need to take over and sort things. This might be for a few minutes, a few days, maybe longer.

There is no moral deficit in dependency itself. All of us go through periods of dependency, like when we are sick or injured, or when we were very young or very old. In some professions, such as aged care or work with people with severe disabilities, dependency is central to the professional relationship, though even there it needs to be managed. In youth work, there will always be elements of dependency. Young people do not have the legal status to take power in some circumstances, and there are many more where their autonomy will not be recognised. They will always be dependent on us to open bank accounts, to organise insurances, to sign for hire vehicles, things like that. But where young people can be put in charge of processes that affect them, they should be.

Conclusion

Empowerment, whether that is the word we use for it or not, is at the centre of ethical youth work. Work that is not empowering is not youth work. This includes *personal empowerment*: enabling a young person's capacity to shape their own 'choice biographies' (Beck 1992), to move closer to becoming the kind of person they want to become. In the terms of the last chapter, this includes the realisation that they have their own power, and that power-holders are not in possession of some mysterious substance called power but exercise a mandate on their behalf. It includes the capacity to hold such people account-able, and to withdraw their power if they so choose; to identify their interests and to act upon them. Empowerment also includes *group empowerment*: the capacity for groups of people to take their place in the common wealth, and to act to remove the barriers or exclusions that unjust social arrangements might put in their way. In the terms of the last chapter, this includes the ability to recognise common interests, and to join with others to bring people together to jointly invest their power in leadership and other delegated functions, to organise for change. It includes *political empowerment*: the capacity to engage in broader decision-making processes, both in one's own interest as a constituent and in the interest of a wider constituency.

Along with any intervention into people's lives goes the risk of creating dependency, in which the person becomes less able to act than they were before. Sometimes, an immediate crisis or risk situation creates circumstances where this is unavoidable. However, while some short-term dependency or high-level sup-port may be necessary to enable young people to get on their feet and be able to take charge of their own lives again, greater agency is always the trajectory.

17

CORRUPTION

Summary

Corruption is defined within this chapter as any action (or omission) by a youth worker which advantages the youth worker at the expense of young people. While we are used to seeing corruption narrowly as involving bribes and relationships with underworld figures, most corruption is more mundane, and much more common than that. The chapter explores what corruption might look like for youth workers, how good people are drawn gradually into corruption, and how it might be avoided.

Corruption is a harsh word. We are used to hearing it used of public officials taking bribes, or siphoning off public money for their own purposes, or unusual relationships between property developers and planning officers or local government councillors. Especially, we would think, in the Third World where systems of governance and accountability aren't well developed and old relationships (or hostilities) take priority over public duty. But corruption is much wider than this, and is by no means confined to exotic places. Corruption can, and does, develop in the most mundane and ordinary of relationships.

Defining corruption

Many definitions of corruption in the literature, like those cited by Garofalo and his colleagues (2001), are context-specific – usually to governments or public officials – so tend to be somewhat limited. A slightly more general definition now used almost universally through the literature is Sarah Rose-Ackerman's elegant formula: 'the misuse of public power for private gain' (1999: 91), or variations on it. Most definitions turn on the conflict between public and private interests. However, we would need to know what is included in public and private interests, and many variants aren't so helpful in understanding the corruption of power that is exercised in the private world, rather than the public one. For example, a father's sexual exploitation of his daughter is undoubtedly a corrupt use of his power, but her interest isn't easily seen as public. A definition of corruption needs to locate it within the power relationship, wherever it occurs, including within the family or informal networks (deLeon and Green 2002). An understanding of corruption thus derives from our understanding of power.

In terms of our discussion in Chapter 15, a power relationship occurs when a constituency gives a mandate to a person to act on their behalf. The person can, however, decide to use that power in a variety of ways:

- to exercise it altruistically to meet the mandate that was given, even in the face of personal loss
- to meet the mandate conscientiously, but to pursue one's own gain also in the process
- to go some way towards meeting the mandate given, but pursue one's own interests rather more energetically and at the expense of meeting the mandate, or even
- to use the power given against the people who gave it.

Corruption involves the last two of these.

Corruption

Is when a person uses the power given by a constituency to further their own interests to the detriment of the interests of their constituency.

The youth work relationship is a power relationship, though one, we would hope, where young people's agency is maintained (see Chapter 16) and where lines of accountability are open. But because it is a power relationship, the possibility of corruption will always be there. And the possibility is not remote. When a youth worker advances themselves at the expense of young people, or uses for their own purposes resources set aside for young people so that they are not available when the young people need them, then that is corruption.

A couple of notes here:

- This definition of corruption does not require that a youth worker not advance themselves (see Chapter 21). Indeed, a lot of the advancement of youth workers will also be in young people's interest. So altruism, acting in spite of one's own interest, isn't required.
- The definition doesn't require that young people be advanced *more* than the youth worker. The youth worker may gain greatly from a line of work, and young people only a small amount.
- The definition does require that a youth worker should not pursue a line of action which will result a greater benefit for them, but a smaller benefit for young people, than would be the case if they took another line of action.

- This is not just about money and other economic goods, but also status and prestige, and various other emotional and psychological goods, such as feeling needed or valuable.
- It isn't just individuals who are subject to corruption. Organisations can too. If a youth work organisation pursues its own interest to young people's disadvantage, then that is corruption (i.e. *institutional* corruption).

Example

Scenario 1. Cathy is in charge of a computer literacy programme at a youth centre. Her organisation has just received a grant to buy 10 computers and she has to organise the purchase. Her own personal computer at home is a bit old and slow. All the local computer shops gave her pretty much the same price for the 10 she had to buy, but she negotiates with one shop to throw in one computer free – for herself. She does the deal with that firm. She doesn't tell her management about the extra computer. She reasons that it was a private deal between herself and the sales person, that the agency still got their 10 computers for the same price, and so it was nobody else's business.

Cathy's rationalisation is wrong here. She isn't a private buyer. She is acting as a delegate for her organisation as well as the young people. The extra computer could be put to use for the young people, even if only as a spare, or used elsewhere in the organisation. Cathy is advancing herself at the expense of the young people. Her reluctance to be transparent should be warning her that her action is probably unethical, and she should be talking to colleagues.

Scenario 2. Exactly the same as Scenario 1, but Cathy lets her management know what she is doing, and they agree to the deal.

Management's sanction doesn't necessarily make any difference: it may not be any less corrupt just because management agrees with it. However, in this case, management is presumably making a judgement on the disadvantage to the young people because of having one less computer versus Cathy's initiative and the advantage to both the organisation and the young people of her being rewarded and having a good personal computer which no doubt she will also use for work. In any case, Cathy's openness makes it ethically safer.

Scenario 3. The shop that was willing to supply the extra computer was slightly more expensive than the others, so she had to accept a slightly less powerful set of computers for the agency in order to get her extra machine.

It seems here that Cathy's action is corrupt, and that management may even be complicit in that corruption if it agreed with the action, unless the judgement is that computing power is not important for what the young people want to do, and/or that the advantage to the young people of Cathy having a good computer at home is significant.

How does corruption work?

It isn't evil people who become corrupt: largely, they don't need to. It is good people, sometimes the best, who become corrupt. People like you. So how does it happen? In the words of one of most the famous aphorisms of all time, 'power corrupts, and absolute power corrupts absolutely' (Lord Acton). A corollary of that could be: 'wherever there is power, there is corruption' (or at least a strong possibility of it). Corruption is *natural* in power relationships. You don't have to work at becoming corrupt; you have to work at not becoming corrupt. This is because each of us sees our own interests rather more vividly and clearly than we see the interests of others. We also understand why our interests are important, and sometimes don't understand so much the importance that other people might attach to things. So, what seems to me to be a balanced and neutral situation, in which my interests are balanced with yours, will most likely be a situation that favours me, not because I am trying to rip you off, but because I know my stuff well and I don't really know yours so well. So, if there is any conflict of interest between a delegate and their constituents, the decision that would seem fair to the delegate is likely to be one slightly tilted in their favour. In other words, where their interests are being met at the expense of the constituency. That is what we have defined as corruption.

Examples

Susan, a detached youth worker, works mostly with young people on the street. She will also do her weekly shopping while at work, dropping it off at home before continuing on her rounds. Is this corrupt?

John is a youth worker in a youth centre. He loves to chat with his friends on the phone while at work, perhaps up to an hour or more a day. He mostly works alone and there often isn't a lot to do. It helps pass the time. Is this corrupt?

Maggie is a keen cyclist. The last four trips away with the young people in her centre have been cycling trips. The young people don't mind, but murmurs of 'Not another cycling trip!' aren't unusual around the centre. Is this likely to be corruption?

James, a keen hill walker and camper, used to be in charge of his youth service's camping programme three or four years ago, but it lost funding. The camping equipment bought through the programme, much of it high quality, was stored in a shed at his home because of fears about security and water damage at the youth centre. There has been a lot of staff and management turnover, and it seems that everybody has forgotten about it. He uses it when he goes out on the weekends with friends or family. Is this corrupt?

Most of the time, the corruption of youth workers will be fairly petty, like the examples above. However, the corruption of good people doesn't usually happen through them being faced with some great moral crisis where they have to either stand up for the right thing or join the dark side. If it did, mostly they would choose the right thing. Usually, at least in the beginning, there aren't any decisions, not big ones anyway. Corruption happens millimetre by millimetre: a decision by a superior that might raise an eyebrow, but oh well, no big deal; an accepted practice in an agency that you get gradually initiated into; a bit of intellectual laziness about something that seems a bit off but you can't be bothered thinking it through or making a fuss. No lines in the sand, no ultimatums, just long slow slippage until you don't really see it as an ethical issue any more – you just got used to it.

While the sorts of issues I'm talking about might be petty in the beginning, corruption is a matter of trajectory. A five degree deviation at the beginning of a journey can leave you hundreds of miles off track by the end of it. There was a situation at the New South Wales Royal Commission of Inquiry into corruption of the police force (1994) where a police sergeant who had just been exposed as deeply corrupt (taking kickbacks and bribes from underworld figures, pocketing money picked up in raids on drug dealers and a whole host of other practices) was asked how it came to this. He told the judge that it had never occurred to him that he was doing anything wrong. Of course, exposed to the clear light of objective analysis, he saw it very clearly indeed and was deeply shocked at where he had ended up.

It is all too easy for practices which advance individuals or agencies at the expense of young people (either particular young people or young people in general) to become normalised, just a part of the way that things are done. Fundraising and involvement with the media is one area that is particularly sensitive.

Examples

Scenario 1. A large charity involved in youth work is heading for its annual fundraising appeal. Knife crime among teenagers is all over the newspapers at this time, although stabbings are actually very rare and declining in number. The charity runs shock television advertisements, using CCTV footage of street brawls among young men, and then cutting to shots of young men talking to the organisation's counsellor or involved in outdoor activities. The fundraising is successful, but the stigmatisation of young people is amplified in their media work. Is this corrupt?

Scenario 2. Reality television shows increasingly feature young people with pathologies of various kinds (drug use, crime, gang membership, laziness or lack of discipline, obesity) and their journey through some kind of youth work intervention. It is good television because some kind of transformation often happens in front of the cameras. A recent UK example was 'Fat Teens In Love'.

(Continued)

(Continued)

The programme used a range of (fundamentally youth work) techniques, including group work, outdoor challenge such as rope work and hiking, and teamwork exercises to build self-esteem and encourage a lifestyle change. The young participants had no doubt agreed to be on television because some others had their faces pixelated out. However, what these young people had effectively consented to was to become the public face of a highly stigmatising condition. Conditions were obviously controlled on the 8-week residential, but not after they returned home.

The organisation involved was given a high profile in the documentary. Judging from the frequency of newspaper and other media appearances recorded on its website, it has a very active and effective media unit.

Is this corruption?

Even if the young person consents, can professionals really give reality shows access to their clients, given that the nature of the professional relationship means that you don't know what is going to happen? And, given a national or international audience, that future repercussions for the young person also cannot be predicted?

Preventing corruption

The greatest danger with corruption is our own capacity for rationalisation and self-deception. Those initial doubts or uncertainties can be easily silenced, while we justify some line of action that some part of us knows isn't in the young people's interest. Learning to pay attention to those doubts, and to check our perception with trusted colleagues, is a critical first step in keeping ourselves, and each other, true to our profession.

A major resource is the kind of culture that we develop within services and teams. Corruption will find fertile ground in teams where conflict is avoided, where criticism or questioning is shut down, where people over-react to a colleague's testing inquiry. It will be more difficult for corruption to find space in teams where people enjoy ethical challenges, where they regularly talk about ethics and participate in training around ethical questions, where asking the question isn't seen as a put down but a genuine and robust attempt to generate better practice and clearer thinking.

This is one place where codes of ethics can be useful. There are lots of questions a code of ethics won't answer. However, they do draw a line in the sand, and my colleagues (and sometimes I) can see when there seem to be a lot of my footprints over the other side of the line.

Corruption flourishes when workers are badly paid, isolated and undervalued (deLeon and Green 2002). In these circumstances, it becomes easy for people to rationalise taking responsibility for their own reward by pursuing their own interest a little too eagerly. The solution is obvious: workers need to be valued, cared for, paid properly, and given access to proper career structures and prospects for personal gain that do not compromise the interests of the young people they work with (see Chapter 21). However, while poor conditions may explain corruption, they don't excuse it. Youth workers are responsible for maintaining their own integrity.

Finally, systems of power have found across the centuries that corruption can only be contained if there are *checks and balances*. There will always need to be other participants, other people with power, who can observe our practice, check our process, pull us up if we are going astray. A single locus of power, whether in a person, a committee, an organisation or a country will always be dangerous. Practice that is unaccountable, where no one knows what the youth worker is doing, will too.

Conclusion

As we have seen, corruption is not just about money, not just about governments, not just about organised crime. Corruption is the dark side of any power relationship, and as productive and important as the youth work relationship is, it is as prone to the abuse of power as any other. For most youth workers, the level of corruption they engage in will be fairly petty. However, unchecked, this trajectory can lead any of us into patterns of decision-making and behaviour that are no different from the general oppression and disregard of young people that we are trying to fight against – perhaps worse. This doesn't take any decision to go over to the dark side: corruption is natural to power relationships. We need to be attentive to our own practice and to that of our colleagues to maintain youth work that has integrity.

18

EQUITY AND JUSTICE

Summary

This chapter deals with ideas about justice and distribution as ethical dimensions of practice, and how they impact on youth work services. We discuss the nature of equality and inequality, working to understand what kinds of equality are legitimate and which ones aren't. The relationship between the treatment of individuals and the treatment of groups is important within this analysis, especially for an understanding of positive discrimination and other anti-oppressive or compensatory practices.

In Chapter 16, I argued that empowerment was at the centre of youth work practice, and that practice which did not at least strive to facilitate and enhance young people's agency could not be ethical, or perhaps could not be youth work. However, empowerment is not alone there, at the centre of our practice. She has a companion, and that companion is justice.

Like empowerment, justice work goes by many names: social justice; equalities work; anti-oppressive practice; anti-racist, anti-sexist, anti-heterosexist work; social change; empowerment; human rights work; advocacy; anti-discrimination, and many others. Very few passages in youth work's history have gone by without one of these terms finding the front of the stage. Many of us feel like we have no choice but to continue to stay in this struggle with and for young people because of the constant experience that where young people are concerned, justice is not done and the requirements of justice not met.

This chapter explores ideas about justice as well as the ethical obligation to attend to justice in our practice: in the services we provide, in our work with institutions, policies, laws and governments, and in young people's dealings with each other and with others in their community.

Justice and discrimination

Definitions of justice are typically deceptively simple. According to formulations reaching back to Plato in the fifth century BC, *justice is about people getting what they deserve* (Campbell 1988). The arguments (and there are many) are about *what* kinds of benefits or burdens should be subject to the requirements of justice, *which people* qualify for consideration in a particular context, and what criteria count when it comes to working out what people *deserve*. There are two forms of justice that are important here.

Commutative justice

The first is concerned with the fair application of sanctions (either rewards or penalties) that arise from the administration of rules or laws. It may have been agreed that a penalty is to be applied if a rule is broken. So, a youth centre might have a rule that anyone who climbs on the roof will be banned from the centre for one session. If a young person climbs on the roof, and they are banned for one session, that is just. If they didn't, but someone said they did, and they are banned, that is unjust. If they did climb on the roof, and they aren't banned, that is also unjust, especially if this is inconsistent and other young people who broke the rule previously have been banned. The fair allocation of rewards and penalties is known as *commutative* justice (Campbell 1988).

A situation where the person or persons deciding on sanctions have already made up their mind on the likelihood that a person has broken the rule is known as *prejudice*. For example, if someone has been climbing on the roof and a particular young person has been known to do that before, and you decide that, on form, it was probably them, even though they deny it and you don't have any evidence to say otherwise.

An important question for processes of commutative justice is whether the rules themselves are fair. For example, a rule might be that anyone who says anything disrespectful to the youth worker will be banned for life. This penalty is disproportionate to the offence, and most of us would say that to carry out such a penalty would be unjust. The distinction here is between *formal* justice and *material* justice. Say a young person called the youth worker an idiot (which, if the youth worker had drafted this rule, might be fair comment) and was then banned for life. They knew the rule, and the rule was strictly and fairly applied. The *formal* requirements of justice have been met. But the rule itself was unfair, so the result is that the young person has no access to the youth service for the rest of their life, which seems unfair. So despite *formal* justice having been satisfied, there is a *material* injustice – the outcome is unjust.

At the broader social level, curfews have sometimes been applied to prevent young people congregating and socialising in public places, for example, in places like Hamilton, Scotland, in 1997 (Thomson 2006), Perth and Port Augusta in Australia, in 1993 and again in 2005, and across a number of US cities in the 1980s and 1990s (Sercombe 1997c). A young person apprehended under curfew law may have no *formal* claim that an injustice had been done. The apprehension may have been precisely in line with the law. However, experience of young people being apprehended and taken into custody just a few yards from their house, at the bus stop where the bus was late, or when they had the express written permission from their parents indicates that *material* injustice was routine. Of course, the US experience that it was mostly black and Hispanic young people who were apprehended also indicated that formal injustice wasn't exactly uncommon either (Sercombe 1997c).

Distributive justice

The second form is to do with the fair distribution of the benefits and burdens of social life. The local bakery might have donated some cakes to the youth centre. A fair distribution would mean that everybody got a piece of cake, or at least the opportunity to have a piece of cake if they wanted one. A situation where some people got several pieces of cake and some didn't get any would be unjust. Or the same group of favoured young people might always be chosen for desirable activities, such as trips away or horse-riding or go-karting. Burdens as well as benefits are important. If some people always do the cleaning up at the end of the night, this would also be unjust. This is known as *distributive* justice, or at the broader social level, as *social justice*.

In a workplace, a situation where young people are paid less for doing the same work as an older person would seem, on the face of it (or, as the philosophers would say, *prima facie*) to be an injustice according to the normal requirements of distributive justice. Although the productivity of the worker might be a *relevant criterion* in deciding how much they should be paid, the age of a worker is not. In fact, there are laws preventing such discrimination against older workers (though not against younger workers), which indicates that the distribution of wage income from the firm should not be based on the age of a worker. If justice is about 'people getting what they deserve', relevant criteria will determine the 'deserve' bit.

Relevant criteria

Depending on the good to be distributed, and on the context, relevant criteria might include:

- rights (e.g. in the allocation of votes)
- wants and tastes (the distribution of music or art)
- ability to pay (the distribution of non-essential material goods)
- physical attractiveness (the distribution of movie roles, modelling jobs or invitations for dates)
- geography (subsidised transport)
- gender (the distribution of cosmetics)
- need (food or medical care)
- religion (the distribution of positions of spiritual leadership)
- disability (the distribution of wheelchairs)
- nationality (positions of public office)
- age (access to dangerous drugs like alcohol and tobacco).

You can probably immediately think of exceptions to all of these, and they might be compelling, but most people would agree that these criteria are relevant for consideration, even if they don't finally determine an outcome.

Discrimination

Distributive justice does not necessarily require that everyone gets the same. If the company in the last example paid different workers a different wage according to experience (assuming that experience affects productivity) or need (so workers with more children get paid more) that would be fine. Both are relevant criteria. But the allocation of benefits or burdens according to irrelevant or arbitrary criteria, such as age, gender, religion, skin colour, ethnic background or 'because I don't like the look of you' is unjust, *prima facie*.

Applying criteria of any sort in the process of distribution is referred to as *discrimination*. Obviously, any act of distribution requires discrimination. Strictly speaking, it is a neutral term. If we are paying according to productivity, we need some mechanism for discriminating between less productive and more productive workers. However, 'discrimination' as a term is mostly used of distributions where the person is being discriminated *against*, using irrelevant or prejudicial criteria. *Positive discrimination* generally refers to the use of irrelevant (*prima facie*) criteria to *advantage* a person because of the likelihood that those same criteria have been used to disadvantage them in the past: in other words, as a form of compensation for past injustices or to rebalance earlier distributions.

What criteria are relevant will depend on the context. In most wage agreements, the individual need of a worker is not a relevant criterion in allocating a wage (except, of course, as a justification for paying young people less. It seems they are always the exception). How many children you have will not usually be taken into consideration. Neither will your gambling habit, or your somewhat oversized mortgage. It is your responsibility to manage your needs in accordance with the standard wage that you might reasonably expect. Whether that ought to be the case is another question, but that's the way it is.

The distribution of health care, however, is different. Here, the individual need of the person is perhaps the only relevant criterion. It would be absurd to allocate each person so many days (and no more) in hospital each year whether they needed them or not. Health care should go to people who are sick, or to prevent them becoming sick.

There may be an issue where a broad range of people might have need but the resource is scarce. The provision of youth work fits this description. Wealthy young people can struggle as much in the process of growing up as anyone does, and often without the kind of connection that youth work can provide. However, the scarcity of youth work resources often means that distribution is *targeted*. It goes to those who are judged to have the most need. Poverty and deprivation are relevant criteria for the distribution of youth work because of the cumulative effect of barriers to participation, which can affect a young person's capacity to find a good life. There are generally more external resources to support a person from more advantageous circumstances. Not that this is in any way reassuring if you happen to be that young person whose family is wealthy but who is personally isolated, cut off from a range of resources, and not managing well.

Equity and equality

This analysis leads to another important distinction: between *equality* and *equity*. Equality means that everyone gets the same. With respect to some goods, such as respect, treatment before the law, or perhaps opportunity of various kinds, equal treatment may indeed be called for. Most basic human rights fall into this category. For others, equal treatment might actually result in injustice. For example, if students in a boarding school all get exactly the same amount of bacon and eggs for breakfast, the little first formers might be stuffed while the great huge sixth formers go hungry. And Jewish and Muslim students potentially don't get anything acceptable to eat at all. Equity, on the other hand, takes account of relevant criteria in order to produce a result that is fair across the various claimants to some good. So each student would get a serving proportional to their needs, with alternatives available to vegetarians or people with religious objections to eating pigs.

Claims that 'everyone is treated the same around here' need to be treated with caution. The question is: what 'same'? Is everyone treated like a new immigrant? Or a Muslim? Or a person with a disability? Or a child? Usually this statement means that everyone is treated as though they were 'mainstream': white, native born, often male. Which means that if you aren't like that, the service you are getting is different, and inferior, from the service that a mainstream person (for whom the service is designed) is getting (Dominelli 2007).

One element of anti-oppressive practice is awareness of difference and openness to the ways in which our standard ways of working might not connect with people who aren't 'mainstream', and, indeed, may reinforce their feeling that they don't belong and their identities, cultures and ways of being are not respected. It is the habit of being watchful and open to our processes and programmes needing to change to accommodate difference. Otherwise, rather than relieving oppression and discrimination, we can amplify it. Conceptions of youth work ethics, including their expression in codes of ethics, generally require that services are provided for young people equitably.

The question of gender is particularly salient here. There is history of girls being ignored in youth services, which have often been initiated to counter the acting-out behaviour of boys. Youth work spaces and activities can be very boy-friendly, which means either that girls don't come or are confined to the margins and to passivity if they do. This is unjust, *prima facie*, according to principles of distributive justice, and requires close and continual attention in our provision.

Objections to the idea of distributive justice

There is an opinion from classical liberal philosophers (notably Friedrich Hayek (1978) and Robert Nozick (1974)) that the very idea of distributive justice is wrong. According to these thinkers, distribution is a random process, made up of the individual economic decisions of millions of producers and consumers. As such, distribution is not an ethical matter: there has never been a decision about how to distribute the goods (and 'bads') of society. If people come by the goods they have legitimately, then those goods are their private property and not subject to claim from other people or, for that matter, from the state. If they didn't come by them legitimately, then that is a matter of commutative justice, not distributive justice.

Distributions of goods obviously do occur, but these are typically a matter of agreement, of contract. If the young worker above has agreed to work for the wage offered, then they can have no complaint that the older worker next to them, who has also agreed to work for the wage being offered to them, is being paid more. If the boss doesn't pay them the agreed wage, then that is a breach of contract and is a matter for the processes of commutative justice enforceable by law. If you don't like it, don't sign the contract.

If distribution is not an ethical matter, neither is redistribution. In fact, these thinkers see redistribution of income or wealth as theft (Hayek 1978). It is up to each of us as individuals to pursue our own interest, and to position ourselves as best we can to get the best share of whatever distributions might be at stake. The relief of suffering might be an ethical matter, but that is not a question of justice, but of compassion, and it is up to each person to determine what compassion, as a virtue, might require of them.

These ideas have been deeply influential in Western capitalist societies. For example, Margaret Thatcher adopted Hayek's *The Constitution of Liberty* as a key manifesto for the Conservative Party (Ranelagh 1991), and the ideas were just as influential in the USA, Australia and New Zealand. The problem is, I think, the extreme individualism of liberal thought: the notion of the freestanding, autonomous person, with no obligations other than those into which he or she has entered by contract. Reaching back as far as Thomas Hobbes (1996, orig. 1651), this idea ignores (or deliberately excludes) how deeply, fundamentally social we are (Koehn 1998). Friedrich von Hayek did not give birth to himself, nor did he suckle at his own breast, choose his own schooling, provide his own meals, or teach himself right from wrong.

Almost every act is a social act, in which decisions about distribution have been made. How much food young Friedrich got, compared with his parents, their dog, or his brothers and sisters, is a question of distribution. It is also a matter of decision: his mother decides at the dinner table how much to put on each plate. This is moral decision-making, a part of what E.P. Thompson (1971) called the 'moral economy'. It is morally wrong for Friedrich to be allowed to starve while his brothers and sisters grow fat. And malnutrition would certainly have had an impact on the development of his ultimately impressive intellect.

To be sure, there is no one person, or even group of persons across a society, who is directing the economic decision about how food is to be distributed in households. But these decisions are nonetheless made in a moral environment that is not random, but patterned by social structure, culture, law and convention (note the number of societies that have routinely fed boys more than girls, with significant implications for their cognitive development). Inequalities are structured into societies in highly patterned ways. And they are cumulative. Friedrich, as a boy, as the child of a doctor and grandchild of academics, already had access to educational opportunities that were not typical of children his age. And access to health care, and various other generous resources on account of his family's wealth (Ebenstein 2001). A mile or two away, there would be other boys and girls struggling to find enough to eat, misshapen by illness or early physical work, unable to go to school. These disadvantages, a result of factors including decisions about the distribution of proportion of income from production in factories and mills and farms that goes to wages, are also patterned, cumulative and intergenerationally transferred. To paraphrase Marx (1935), Friedrich von Hayek certainly made his own history – he made choices and worked hard and wrote books – but under pre-established conditions which had come down from the past.

As a matter of fact, irrelevant criteria have often been applied to distributive decisions. Gender, for example, with a discounted share of income going to women, either through direct discrimination or through low pay in occupations dominated by women. People from minority ethnic groups have either been excluded from employment or confined to low-paying jobs. The wrong accent, the wrong look, the wrong age, can all result in significantly lower returns from your labour. This does not only apply to income, though. Many other goods, such as education, health care, travel, entertainment and access to political representatives may all be dependent on income, and therefore cumulative. In other words, if you have a good income, you get all of these, and if you don't, you don't get any. For each distributive decision made according to irrelevant criteria, there is an accusation of unfairness that must be met, and a case for compensation if the accusation stands.

In many cases, this is not just about individuals, or even families. Whole towns have borne the brunt of discriminatory decision-making with respect to the provision of health care. Whole races of people have lived under discrimination in employment or access to education. The burdens of this are often intergenerational: the wholesale exclusion of Aboriginal children in Australia from elementary schooling from the 1930s to the 1950s (Haebich 1992) meant that their children also lived in educationally-poor households, and many of their grandchildren as well. We know that the educational environment at home is strongly predictive of educational success, which impacts on income and economic status. A grandchild so burdened clearly has a legitimate claim, even if they were not themselves formally excluded from education. Whole populations become deprived through such distributive decisions, and whole populations also become advantaged. It is this logic that has led to the practice of *positive discrimination*.

Positive discrimination

There is a core tension at the heart of the notion of positive discrimination, with roots that are ancient and cross-cultural. It is about the extent to which we treat people as individuals, and the extent to which we treat them as members of groups. Theorists refer to this as principles of collective justice versus individual justice (Patterson 1992).

In many cultures, a person is first of all a member of their community, and secondarily an individual (Imam 1999). What is true of the community as a whole is true of them as an individual: whatever they do, they do as a member of their community, and are seen by others that way. Everyone in the community is therefore a participant in their activity (the community did, after all, bring them up) and they are a participant in the actions of everyone else. We are familiar with this, especially in collective events like the Olympics, where we get quite excited by how many medals 'we' have won, all the while, of course, sitting firmly on our sofa.

Say someone in the community commits a crime. In a society in which notions of collective justice are strong, if the actual individual who did the crime cannot be identified or found, justice will be satisfied by exacting a punishment on a relevant and appropriate alternative member of their community – a brother, say (Patterson 1992). This will be very familiar to workers who work with young people in gangs or any structure where there is strong collective identification. If a rival gang knows that one of the Partick Young Team did the deed, but they don't know which one or can't get to him, any one of the Team will do.

This may seem offensive to a liberal tradition with a strong view of an individual's responsibility for their own action. It seems unjust to punish someone who didn't themselves do anything wrong but is part of a community including someone who did. But notions of collective responsibility are ancient, well developed and well understood in many societies. They are also pretty primal, lying very close to the surface of even the most liberal of us.

Positive discrimination deals with the fact that even in supposedly liberal societies like ours, where each person is supposedly treated on their merits, collective practices abound. Decisions are made about young people, ethnic minorities, particular religious groups, women, working-class people and others as though they were all the same. The treatment of such groupings has historically often been profoundly unjust. When this is realised at a later point in time, things are often at the point where unjust and discriminatory practices are institutionalised, prejudices are embedded in the culture, disadvantages are multigenerational and cumulative, and the whole thing is a big mess. Generally, it isn't enough just to stop the discriminatory behaviour because the consequences of past discrimination live on. Positive discrimination tries to deal with the mess by favourable treatment of individuals who are members of groups who were previously treated unfavourably.

The difficulty is that this kind of compensatory action at the group level can look and feel a lot like injustice at the individual level. There is no real problem if the good being distributed is not scarce, or if access to it is not competitive. Access to bank loans at low interest for disadvantaged groups might be an example. Nobody much is disadvantaged by that. Where the goods are scarce and access is competitive, it becomes more difficult. Positive discrimination may mean that a person who is a member of a 'mainstream' group is passed over for a job or a university place, even though they may be more qualified. It may also be true that they, *as an individual*, have never really experienced much of the advantage supposedly accruing to a member of their group, and indeed that the person from a minority group who got the job may have had a very privileged background and never experienced prejudice *as an individual* even though they are a member of a targeted, generally disadvantaged group.

It is difficult, but necessary, to hold the requirements of justice for both individuals and groups in tension. We are individuals, responsible for our own behaviour and liable for our own misdeeds. According to notions of collective responsibility, we are also members of families, groups, communities and nations, and bear collective responsibility for the actions of people in our families, groups, communities and nations, even though we may strongly disagree with those actions. My generation may have the responsibility to compensate for the injustices perpetrated by my grandparents' generation, for example. Many young people understand this explicitly, especially if they come from communities with strong collective identity, such as Aboriginal groups, gangs, sectarian communities or religious minorities. Justice work with young people requires an understanding of this reality.

Ethics of care

For some theorists, justice is *the* ethical principle, subsuming and 'trumping' other ethical requirements (Campbell 1988). This has come in for some serious criticism, especially by feminist philosophers like Carol Gilligan (1997) and Nel Noddings (2002; see also Muuss 1996; Koehn 1998), who have argued that views of justice which look for abstract and universal principles in order to make objective judgements about right and wrong represent a 'male' way of thinking, a male preference for arms' length relationships and ambivalence about emotional expressiveness (Koehn 1998). But human beings are embedded in relationships: real, intimate, emotional relationships. Human beings who are put together properly *care*. Care, the process of listening to another's world and understanding why things are that way for them, understanding what they need or are asking for, is a deep and powerful ethical driver which may conflict with the objective and abstract determinations of justice.

For some feminist theorists, the ethic of care has been ignored or diminished by the work of male theorists of justice, such as Kant, Rawls and John Stuart Mill. For Gilligan (1997) and her colleagues, care, empathy and the process of connection with another human being is central to ethical behaviour, and may indeed be the ground of all ethical behaviour.

Daryl Koehn's 1998 book *Rethinking Feminist Ethics* traces over this thinking. She is sympathetic to these claims, but also argues that care, by itself, is not enough. As we noted in Chapters 16 and 17, care itself can become corrupted, serving the need of a person to care rather than the need of the person cared for. Care also does not carry within itself the mechanisms needed to regulate, limit and hold it accountable. Care can end up being evil if it is manipulative, suffocating or over-invested in those that one cares for at the expense of others who may be unknown to you but deeply affected by the behaviour of those who are close.

Koehn concludes that while care is critical as a component of ethical decision-making, care is not enough by itself to establish a basis for ethics. Accepting the need to consider the viewpoints of everyone affected by decision-making, she argues that the requirements of justice are not 'trumped' by care any more than the requirements of care are 'trumped' by justice. Ethical decision-making is *dialogical*, a process of engaging with the perspectives of all involved, including their reasonable expectations that people obey laws, respect property and respect people's right to make decisions about their own lives perhaps over and against what others may want or even need them to do. Justice and care have always corrected each other's excesses.

Example

There is a rule in a youth centre that anyone using racist insults will be banned for a period of time. On this particular day, there is a conflict in the youth centre between two young people, and one uses a racist insult to the other. However, the youth worker knows that this young person is regularly being bullied by an ethnically identified gang, has a range of other distressing things going on in their lives at the moment, and has limited supports. The youth worker is inclined not to enforce the rule. What would you advise?

The ethics of social action

A consistent theme throughout this book has been that young people are one of those groups subjected to unfair discrimination. A lot of our work goes into dealing with the consequences of this discrimination, and the compounding effects of other discriminatory statuses like geography, ethnicity, language group, or class. Youth practice that takes ethics seriously cannot be comfortable with cleaning up the consequences of injustice while allowing injustice to continue. From the beginning, the best youth work has been committed to advocating for young people not only to secure adequate youth work provision, but to address structural injustices in the way that major institutions deal with young people, the way that policy impacts on young people, the way that laws discriminate against young people or allow discrimination to occur.

> ### Example
>
> A detached youth work agency, new to the estate, was shocked by what seemed to be routine practices by police of gathering confessions or information about crimes from young people through the use or threat of violence. The agency organised a pager-linked call-out service staffed by volunteers to provide an independent adult witness when young people were arrested or questioned. The agency also provided support for young people who wanted to complain about having been assaulted by police. While no official sanctions against police officers ever resulted from inquiries into these allegations, the knowledge that events would be officially reported and recorded soon resulted in a sharp decline in the incidence of police violence in the area. The presence of an independent adult witness made sure that due process was followed in questioning.

So youth work does not always mean work with young people. It might mean work *for* young people. It is possible to be a youth worker and not be in any contact with young people at all, though in the interests of actually knowing young people's situation you wouldn't want that to continue for too long. As well as working face to face with young people, youth work practice is also training youth workers, managing youth services, doing research, studying, writing youth policy, responding to youth policy, organising political action, doing work with parents or schools… as long as young people are the primary client and you are concerned with them in their social context.

This has not always been carried through into our understanding of who is a youth worker and who isn't. We have often excluded policy workers, researchers, managers, academics, perhaps even politicians. Other professions don't do this. A lawyer doesn't cease being a lawyer because they happen to be working for the United Nations on human rights policy. A doctor doesn't cease being a doctor because they are now doing cancer research and spending most of their time in the lab or at conferences. The particular training and skill set of youth workers means that moving up through the ranks isn't unusual for people in our field. There are lots of people in important positions who were at one time youth workers. However, rather than claiming these as our own, maintaining contact and supporting their continuing commitment to young people, we tend to see them as having left the profession once they have moved out of face-to-face contact. This can also mean that the profession is constantly suffering brain drain as talented people move up and out into other roles.

Conclusion

The requirements of justice are close to the centre of what youth work is trying to do. However, youth work has not always been sensitive to the ways in which its own practice has reproduced injustices that exist within the communities in which young people live, let alone challenge the injustices that flourish outside the youth work space. This chapter has drawn on core ethical theory about justice to make sense of concepts of equality and equity, social or distributive justice, positive discrimination, and the need for attention to fairness in the application of rules and sanctions within spaces for which we are responsible.

These are not only issues within the youth work space, in relationships between young people, and in their relationships within their immediate neighbourhood. A sustained youth work ethics requires attention not only to young people's personal development and their relationships with each other and within their immediate communities, but also to the social structures that produce systems of inequality, exclusion, poverty and deprivation in the neighbourhoods within which youth services are often placed.

The ethical commitment to change in structures that impact unjustly on young people means that any youth service which is only concerned with personal development in the young people they are working with is only dealing with half the story. It may not be unethical not to be involved in working for social change, but the reality of routine injustice against young people means that there is an ethical gap in our practice if it is not being attended to. Involvement in campaigns like lowering the voting age, equal pay for equal work, young people's rights to be in public space, reform in the secondary school curriculum, living incomes for students, and the place of young people in unions should be included in the strategic plans of every youth service. If it isn't, the challenge of commentators like Rob White (1990; Poynting and White 2004) that youth workers are often just soft cops, and documents like the Jasper Declaration (National Youth Workers Conference 1977) 'that we are content to deal solely with the casualties rather than delving deeply into the cause of those casualties' continue to call us to account.

19

WORKING ETHICALLY ACROSS DIFFERENCE

Summary

Cross-cultural work, or working across difference, is typical within the youth work field, and is becoming more so the more globalised the world becomes. Ethical practice in the face of sometimes striking cultural difference is more complex than in a single cultural environment (if any such thing exists). In the face of prejudice and negative discrimination routinely experienced by members of minority groups, it is all the more necessary to think critically and reflectively about our practice, especially the often unconscious tendency to prefer our own kind, to see our ways as superior, our arrangements as normal, our people as better, and our cultures as more advanced or progressive.

The last chapter dealt with the core principles of justice and their implications for ethical youth work that takes equity seriously. Working equitably at the level of youth work provision requires intelligence, sensitivity and subtlety. Not recognising a young person's collective identification, as a Maori, as a young woman, as a Catholic, as gay, as a member of the Partick Young Team, as Asian or a person with a disability may lead to a person not feeling recognised as a person and all sorts of insensitivity and offence in the youth work encounter. On the other hand, a young person may want those other identities to be ignored, and to try out different ways of being in the youth work space that they don't have access to elsewhere: ways of being that are not about having a disability, or being a Catholic. In some settings, for example where racial or sectarian conflict is common, it may be blessed relief that here, at least, who they are is not overdetermined by the fact of being Catholic or Protestant. Girls may want to play pool or football, rather than do art or make-up.

Identities are complex. All of us carry multiple identities: identities of age, gender, cultural background, sexuality, nationality, physicality and appearance, class, religion, generation, regionality, rurality/urbanity, ethnicity, race, linguistic background, any of which can be mixed. The golfer Tiger Woods, for example, doesn't identify as black, pointing to his Irish, Native American, Thai and Chinese ancestries as equally significant (Kamiya 1997). Which identity is most powerful at any time, and how a young person wants to be seen, might not be predictable. At the same time, any or all of these identities or identifications can shape, constrain, protect, promote or exclude us.

We all work with stereotypes. In fact, the inability to use stereotypes is socially incompetent. Treating a 14 year-old boy the same as their 60 year-old grandmother is just stupid, and probably disrespectful to both. Our first encounters with anybody are shaped by our assessment of the 'kind of person' they are. According to symbolic interactionist theory (see Cuff et al. 1998: Chapter 6), all of us shape our own appearance according to the 'kind of person' we want to be perceived as being. None of this is purely individual: we not only choose, but are also allowed certain identities by the society in which we live. I might feel like a 25 year-old, and want to be seen as a 25 year-old, but the fact is that I am not 25 and that isn't going to happen. Skilful work around identity and stereotype recognises the symbolic indicators of identity that a person is displaying, but also notices subtle contradictions, picks up cues about how a person might want to stretch or play with their identity a bit more. Above all, a skilful communicator keeps the question of identity and stereotype flexible and fluid, open to negotiation, change and play. Facilitating agency means working with people within and beyond their surface identities.

Youth work has not always done this well. Often, youth work has been chauvinistic (i.e. believing that people like ourselves are superior to people who are different) and imperialistic (working to assimilate people of difference into the dominant culture or make them compliant to the dominant culture (National Youth Workers Conference 1977)). Often, funding bodies have required youth workers to 'work on' young people from different class or ethnic cultures to bring them into line with what the authorities expect; and too often, youth workers have obeyed.

Still, how can a youth worker avoid work which may have the best of motives, but turns out on reflection to be oppressive?

Can a white worker work with black young people?

One of the ways to address the danger of cultural imperialism in our work (or, in other words, to promote *cultural safety*) is to employ youth workers who are from the same cultural background (Sallah and Howson 2007). Cultural safety (Papps and Ramsden 1996) is something that mainstream people rarely have to face, except when they travel to places where they are in the minority *and* their privileged status as a Westerner or a tourist or a white person doesn't count for anything.

Young people from minority cultures have to live with cultural risk all the time, especially when their identities are visually discernable. Even where the social context is supposed to be sympathetic, they can never relax. At the very least, they have to be alert all the time to people saying stupid or offensive things, and to know how they are going to deal with that: to let it go and implicitly condone it, to correct it and have to enter into long explanations, or to go on the attack. This gets very tiresome, and there can be social penalties if they get it wrong. Youth spaces should be somewhere where they don't have to do this, where they can just *be*. But they rarely are.

The presence of a youth worker from the same background as them can be a massive relief. For once, they can just rely on someone in power to take over the education of an ignorant and offensive mainstream and they can get on with their planning meeting or their game of pool. If they get it wrong, or lose their cool, they can rely on someone who they know understands to defend them.

Culturally-specific workers often know communities that young people are from, or can access them easily, enabling lines of intervention which would be difficult for mainstream workers. Their own cultural knowledge is often deep and instinctive – they just 'know what to do'.

There are other advantages too, some of them not directly to do with how well a worker does their job.

- Mainstream young people get to see minority people in desired, attractive roles. It becomes harder for people from the mainstream to diminish people from a minority group when one of your favourite people is 'one of them'.
- Minority young people also get to see one of their people in desired, attractive roles. This can elevate their own sense of self-respect. Poverty of aspiration is a common feature of stigmatised peoples, and is a major target of good youth work. Minority youth workers can address it just by being there.
- Because of unfair discrimination, good jobs can be hard to find for people from stigmatised minorities, and specialist or 'identified' positions in youth work or other human services can be one place where this discrimination is redressed.
- Poverty and disadvantage often go along with minority status. A professional income is often not only a resource for the person employed in that position, but for the community from which they come (Sercombe 2008). A white worker taking a specialised position working with black young people represents a deduction from the economy of that community. In order for the employment of a white worker to be justified, they have to be that much better than a black worker from a broader point of view of distributive justice.

All of these elements are not just to do with effectiveness, but have ethical importance. All of them go to the question of distributive justice for people of difference. However, again, the situation is not simple, and one size definitely doesn't fit all.

For example, perhaps because of histories of educational disadvantage, qualified workers from a given minority background may be hard to find. There is certainly justification for employing underqualified workers and training them into positions. But young people whatever their background need youth workers to be skilled, trained and professional. A minority background is not a sufficient qualification to be a good youth worker. Placing a worker in a demanding position for which they haven't been trained also isn't fair to the worker (Imam 1999).

Youth work agencies need to be in consultation with minority communities to determine what their young people need. It may be that the community wants skilled and sympathetic mainstream workers to help their young people integrate into mainstream institutions and adapt to mainstream ways of life.

> ### Example
>
> A youth service was operating in an area with a very high Vietnamese population. However, despite that, there were no Vietnamese young people using the service. All the workers were Anglo, which might have had something to do with it. (The situation where there is discriminatory effect, even without any intention to discriminate, is known as *structural discrimination*. There may not be any exclusionary processes going on, but the absence or under-representation of certain populations is good *prima facie* evidence that something exclusionary is happening.) The agency saw this as an ethical problem.
>
> Workers and management took this problem to the local Vietnamese community, talking over several months. It might have been the case that Vietnamese young people didn't need any kind of youth work service, that the functions of youth work could have been met more than adequately in their families and communities, and the Project didn't want to impose. However, the community felt strongly that they needed some intervention with their young people, and wanted the Project to sponsor that. Although it was an Anglo service, community leaders felt that a service internal to the Vietnamese community would find it hard to work across the divisions that existed within the community itself, so it would be difficult for a service which was internal to the Vietnamese community to be equitable.
>
> Jointly, the Project and the community applied for funding and employed a Vietnamese worker. However, the Anglo workers also took familiarisation lessons in the Vietnamese language, and worked alongside the Vietnamese worker, who also worked extensively with Anglo young people.

The employment of minority specialist youth workers can also ghettoise the practice, leaving minority workers to work with minority young people and the rest of us to stay in our comfort zone. This is also not ethically adequate. As the next chapter will argue, self-knowledge and self-development are an ethical obligation for all professionals, including youth workers. If you work in an area with a high minority population, or even if you have significant contact with a single young person from a minority background, it is incumbent on you to learn what you can, and what you need to, in order to give the young person what they need.

Intervening with young people's attitudes

The young people that we work with have often grown up in highly racialised, sectarian or macho cultures. While they may have been subject to unfair discrimination and injustice themselves, it is not unusual to hear young people reproducing attitudes which denigrate other social groups, put down women, engage in sexist or racist or homophobic banter and more serious forms of hate speech. Occasionally, this can spill into physical violence, and active exclusion of people with a particular identity from access to the service.

Engaging young people as our primary client does not mean acceptance of everything they say and do. It is critical that all young people who need it have access to the kind of support that youth work can provide, and that everyone engaged in a youth work process can feel safe within it – which might mean safe from other young people. This may require intervention. There are a number of ways to do this.

One is to promote a general ethic of respect. Disrespectful language or behaviour is sanctioned actively and consistently within the youth work space, and young people actively learn what constitutes disrespect. One youth centre I worked in had a four-foot high capital R on the wall of the main room, which everyone understood was for 'Respect'. If interactions of any kind got out of line, young people and workers would just raise an eyebrow and point to the 'R'. It wasn't always enough, but often it worked fine. It did facilitate a fairly low-key intervention where language started to get prejudicial. More formal sessions or workshops working with themes around tolerance, race, self-awareness and stereotyping might be indicated from time to time.

In some cases, identity-specific nights or spaces for particular groups, such as young women or Muslim young people, might be a way to create opportunity for groups which may not feel comfortable with a generic space. There is some risk of creating backlash by mainstream groups who may not have access at those times, and this needs to be managed. Even a backlash can provide opportunity for discussion and understanding if worked with well.

Conclusion

All of these approaches, even if low key, are asserting a particular value stance. This is that unfair discrimination against anyone is unjust, and that dealing with all human persons with respect is a core ethical principle upon which our practice (and hopefully our lives) is based. This position does not accept that all value stances have equal merit, and suggests that the racism of young people can't be endorsed or condoned. The reality of difference is one thing. The interpretation and promotion of understandings of difference in stigma, into verbal, emotional and physical violence are not something that youth work can allow to happen in any space within which we have influence.

Beyond that, we need to be aware of our own racism or other prejudice. A preference for people like ourselves, and the slide into seeing others in negative terms (even unconsciously), is something most people have to work against. Ethical practice means constantly educating ourselves and each other, staying open and generous, and remaining humble about our own cultures and traditions in the face of the kaleidoscope of human life that we come across in our day-to-day work.

20

PROFESSIONAL DEVELOPMENT

Summary

A commitment to training is a feature of all professions. Our field is complex and constantly changing, and to be able to intervene in ways that work, that avoid further harm, and are flexible and creative, we need to attend to our own development and training. Initial training is important, but it isn't enough. And all codes of ethics require a commitment to ongoing professional development as well as initial training. This chapter addresses these questions, including whether specified training ought to be mandatory for people calling themselves youth workers.

The ethical duty to take responsibility for continuing professional education is taken up by almost every code of ethics in every profession. It is a feature of all the youth work codes of ethics as well, and for good reason. Youth work is an intervention into the lives of young people – sometimes a serious intervention, with long-lasting results. Caring is not enough: you have to be good at what you do, have good information at your fingertips, know what you are talking about. Your skills need to be up to scratch, ready to deal with anything from conflict between young people to someone having an epileptic fit to using social networking software. The commitment to professional development has double force: professional development develops you as a person, as an individual. It also makes you wiser, more skilled and more flexible as a practitioner, and makes a wider range of resources available to the young people you work with. The evidence is also that continuing professional development has a strong impact on staff retention (Hartje et al. 2008).

The world does not stay the same. Along with a changing world, knowledge about the world and frameworks for understanding it change too. Young people need us to be knowledgeable of the information they need, across a wide range of subjects – from the effects of certain drugs to what happens in pregnancy to cycles of domestic violence. In order to be adaptive to the changing policy and funding environment (and hopefully to influence it), we need to be aware of trends and movements in politics and in bureaucratic discourse.

Youth workers don't need to know everything (though they need to have the skills to find out quickly). But as generalists, they need to know a lot, and as their careers progress, that body of knowledge ought to be growing. By mid-career, you ought to be a pretty impressive body of knowledge yourself. That means reading and research, taking courses and being on the lookout for new ones, attending conferences and seminars, deciding to enrol in a postgraduate certificate or diploma or Masters degree. Or taking the plunge and going back for a PhD.

There are many more opportunities for training and development for youth workers than was once the case, especially in formal educational institutions. Thirty years ago, there were only a handful of tertiary programmes in youth work in the world – I don't think there were any, at degree level, let alone Masters or above. Now, degree-level qualifications are standard for entrants to youth work in the UK, and diploma-level at least in Australia, with many youth workers degree-trained. Bachelor degree-level training is also available in the USA and Canada, and is in the process of being rolled out in New Zealand.

The downside of this is that pre-service training is sometimes seen as enough, with the consequence that your degree is the last bit of training you ever do. The availability of tertiary or post-secondary courses can also lead to a decline in the availability of short-course training opportunities, as employers rely on pre-service training to do the job for them, get complacent about continuing professional development for their workforce, and stop investing in ongoing training.

A lot of the responsibility for facilitating your ongoing professional development rests with your employers and/or managers. Good managers are on the lookout for development opportunities for their staff, outside the sector as well as inside. Budgets ought to include a serious component for continuing professional development (CPD), and managers need to be prepared to spend it. CPD should be seen as essential, and as a right for workers, not an optional add-on. Supervisors need to be attentive to gaps in a worker's development, opportunities to further refine their strengths, and experiences which will keep them moving, keep them fresh, keep them flexible.

What do we need? Thinking creatively about professional development

It is a temptation to see professional development (PD) narrowly, as concerned only with the development of technical or procedural skills that are immediately applicable to the current work process. These are important. IT skills, first aid, awareness of policies and procedures are all necessary. But youth work runs principally on the quality of its imagination. Professional development needs to pay attention also to developing the imagination and creativity of workers, honing their intelligence, learning new theory or new frameworks for understanding old problems.

There is frequently a problem with the availability of good quality, relevant professional development. All of us have sat through irrelevant, boring PD that was an expensive waste of time. Agencies or worker networks might need to take the initiative, deciding what the training needs are for workers in a locality or a field of practice or an organisation, and recruiting trainers or facilitators to deliver it. It may even be better to nominate someone from within the community of practice, one of yourselves, to develop curriculum and deliver the development experience. It is by no means always the case that someone from outside can do the job better than you can yourselves.

Examples of ideas-driven professional development

There might have been an increase in Chinese immigrant settlement in your patch. What about getting someone from the local Temple to help you understand the particular variant of Buddhism that these young people might be connected with?

Could you invite a sociologist from the local university to talk about what is new and interesting in social theory that might be relevant to working with young people? As Kurt Lewin said, 'there is nothing so practical as a good theory' (Lewin 1951: 169).

Or someone from another profession, say social work or psychology or medicine or policing, to talk about the latest developments in their field that might have implications for young people?

Or someone from another field in our profession: someone who works with cared-for young people, or young people with disabilities, or mental health issues, or alcohol and other drug counselling?

What about a webcam link with someone in South Africa or Finland to share developments in youth work practice in their region?

Or getting someone from the youth wing of a political party to discuss how policy is developing behind the scenes in their party with respect to young people?

Or lining up a half-hour telephone conversation with some interesting thinker from the USA or Germany or Bolivia to discuss a paper of theirs that you have all read?

Should pre-service training be mandatory?

This is a live question across a range of different jurisdictions. It is also an ethical question. The claim to be a youth worker, or employment as a youth worker, gives a person privileged access to young people. It signals to young people that this is someone they should be able to trust, that they shouldn't need to have their guard up.

In terms of whether this trust is warranted, the intention of any person to help young people is a good start. However, youth work is more than care, more than liking young people and being concerned for them and wanting to help. As Koehn has argued (1998), care can be misguided, distorted or corrupted, and is no guarantee against harm. Youth work has developed strong traditions of *how* care happens in the youth work context, which have been developed in earlier chapters of this book and in foundational documents such as the Albemarle Report (Ministry of Education 1960) and Bernard Davies' *Manifesto* (Davies 2005). These do not come naturally, and are not necessarily common sense (indeed, given how prejudicial common sense is towards young people, they may be directly counter to common sense). For the kind of care and concern that a person has for young people to be styled *youth work*, there needs to be a process of induction into these traditions.

This does not necessarily need to happen through formalised, accredited training. For those of us who became youth workers before the existence of such training, that wasn't a possibility anyway. We learnt informally, by working with more experienced youth workers and figuring it out as we went along. However, there is a question of quality control here. I began my career (unintentionally, largely) as a youth worker as an 18 year-old, within an established youth work organisation, as part of a team. I spent a year and a bit working there, with good training and support (for the late 1970s!). Then I was working on my own, as a detached youth worker in a single-worker agency, with a volunteer supervisor and committee who were as inexperienced in youth work as I was, though generally somewhat wiser. I also had the luxury of enrolment in a one-day-a-week unaccredited community work course run by a faith-based organisation, which offered some support and training.

I think that generally I was a good youth worker. But I look back now, 30 years on, and certain events and practices make me cringe. Nobody died, and I don't think that anybody suffered permanent harm – I hope not, anyway. However, with respect to the former, they easily could have. I took groups of young people on adventure-type weekends, often with me as the only worker, with inadequate equipment, in sometimes harsh environments. I had no first aid training, nor was there anyone else in the group who did. It was good luck, rather than good management, that nobody came to grief. With respect to permanent harm, I'm not so sure. I can think of a number of encounters or ways of dealing with young people that were not good, and where I cannot at all be confident that no significant damage ensued. If I was my supervisor at any of those points, I would have had serious words.

I am sure that many people who enter youth work without formal pre-training do an exemplary job, and have good instincts about how to work developmentally with young people and where the boundaries to the youth work relationship are. Many have the privilege of working with experienced youth workers who are masters of their profession and great mentors to new inductees. Many, however, don't. Many (like me) pick it up over time, eventually get some training by slow accumulation of short courses or seminars, or eventually go back to university. In the meantime, we practised on young people without any real oversight of our work. We made our mistakes on them.

Of course, you will always make mistakes. I went back to ground-level youth work practice seven years ago, after 25 years in the field and 15 as a lecturer, and still made lots of mistakes, including some very silly ones. But core training, including training in ethics, creates a kind of cushion which protects young people at least from the routine and predictable distortions of intervention as well as the outright outrageous ones.

There is no question that it is an ethical obligation for youth workers, including volunteers, to train and to continue to seek training. On that there is consensus. Whether a person should not be allowed to practise as a youth worker until some core training has been completed is more controversial. What that core training should be is even more so. The conditions under which a person engages with young people are critical here, especially the supervisory context, the amount of responsibility or autonomy, and the extent to which the person is working alone. On balance, I think that nobody should be able to use the title of youth worker without core training, and nobody should be able to work with young people as a youth worker unsupervised without a recognised qualification. We tend not to use terms like 'youth work assistant' for volunteers, students or trainees, but this could be useful as a way to indicate to young people the degree to which a person has taken on the profession, and to what degree they can expect a professional youth work relationship with them.

Professional development – and development of the profession

The other side of professional development is the responsibility and initiative we take for the development of our own profession. Since the Hippocratic Oath, the ethics of the professions has included the obligation to give back to those who gave to you, to help develop others as others have developed you. We often look to governments to support this process. However, this profession, to which we are committed, was begun and continues to live because ordinary citizens had a concern for young people among them, and sought to connect and converse with those young people. The development of the profession is also not primarily the responsibility of governments, but the responsibility of youth workers.

There are a number of ways that we, as youth workers, should be taking responsibility for the development of our profession:

1. Supervision of student placements.
2. Mentoring workers who are new to the field.
3. Recruiting people who would make good youth workers.
4. Writing and publishing.
5. Conducting, and publishing, practice-based research, including writing up demonstration projects, innovative approaches and action research.
6. Developing field-based CPD courses, further education and tertiary training.

7. Engagement with the media.
8. Resourcing organisations that support the development of youth work as a profession, including youth work representative bodies and unions.

Time and space do not allow for a full development of this discussion beyond this list. But the investment of time in one or more of these should be part of the portfolio of individual youth workers and youth work organisations, recognised as a legitimate part of our work and supported by employers and funding bodies. If this support is not forthcoming, we need to be doing it anyway, in our own time if necessary. This is part of our commitment to the ethical development of our profession. Especially, *we need to be prepared to pay subscriptions to professional organisations or unions at a level that will give them the capacity for advocacy independent of government* and if necessary, to take issue with government when required.

Things to consider

- What are you doing right now to support the development of your profession?
- If you are new to the profession, who are the people around you who are helping develop youth work as a profession?
- Where can you see a role for yourself in the future?
- How much would you be prepared to pay, per annum, in membership fees to a professional youth work organisation? How would this compare to your car insurance bill?

Conclusion

Training does not make you a professional. Rather, because you are a professional, you make sure you are trained. As we discussed in Chapter 2, being a youth worker is a matter of your fundamental ethical commitment to the service of young people. But if you are a youth worker, you will make sure that you continue to stay abreast of the skills, knowledge, theories, research and ideas that young people might need and that you might need in order to do your job. This may not be initiated or even resourced by your employer. Some employers are painfully unaware of this need, don't make proper provision for it, or don't spend the provision that they do make. However, your obligation is not contingent on their support. With or without employer support, continuing professional development is part of the practice of ethical youth work. The only qualifier to the question 'read any good books lately?' should be whether the books you have read were good, not whether you have read any.

21

NOW ABOUT YOU: SELF-CARE

Summary

The most important resource that youth workers have in the service of young people is their own selves: their minds, bodies, emotions, perceptions, personalities. In order for this service to be at the level that young people need and deserve, youth workers need to pay attention to their own health and a proper life balance. This is especially so since there are traditions within our field that promote over-commitment and unsustainable work practices.

In Chapter 4, we discussed the range of motivations that youth workers have, and particularly motivations which were not about the youth worker's own self-interest. We argued there that the service professions were inherently 'other-directed': that they existed not primarily to serve the interests of the practitioner, but of the client or client group. However, descriptions of our motives as 'altruistic' weren't necessarily useful, if altruism means service in which the motives are *totally* other-directed, and in which no attention is paid to the youth worker's own needs. Koehn (1994) argues that this kind of 'pure' altruism is in fact unstable: that while occasional acts of pure altruism are fine (and probably necessary), after a time, the chances are that a worker becomes increasingly resentful and bitter about the amount of effort they were putting in 'without being appreciated'.

On the other hand, we argued in Chapter 17 than meeting one's own needs *at the expense of* young people was corrupt, and that vigilance was needed to prevent an often indiscernible, natural slide into self-interest and corruption over time.

Alongside both of these points is the fact of life that being a youth worker can be hard. You can be working at all hours of the day, for not much money (or none at all), with people who are a bit broken and a bit difficult, in situations which can be objectively dangerous and stressful. Supervisory or proper management support can be seriously lacking, the job can be insecure due to funding instability, the resources you need to do the job well aren't there, and you can come under attack from local authorities or community members or police or the media who associate you with the problems you are trying to solve.

At times, organisational or professional cultures can revel in this kind of hardship, developing a kind of victim identity or a culture of masochism where the suffering of the worker is the measure of the work. Organisations can churn through workers, especially volunteers or quasi-volunteers, appealing to their compassion or faith or political idealism to secure a commitment to the work that is not rewarded or even supported financially or professionally, and for which no training is offered.

For some people, this can be a real awakening, an insight into the workings of a society that they could never have got access to by themselves, and they move on to other work psychologically stronger, a bit older and a lot wiser. For some, it can be an entry point to a longer, more sustained youth work engagement somewhere else, the beginning of a career. For some, it results in burnout, damage, bitterness and cynicism. It is not unusual for the latter to be greeted with condemnation and finger-wagging by the organisation, locating the failure in the worker's own moral or psychological inadequacies.

Most youth work agencies are not like that. But it is not unusual, even in the most enlightened of organisations, to find some elements of this culture not very far under the surface.

There is a key principle here: that the youth worker is also a person. The youth worker is also deserving of ethical consideration, not just as a source of ethical action, but also as a recipient: a person about whom decisions are made, who needs resources to be distributed to them, and who needs to be cared for in the process of their work. This is not just the responsibility of third parties like managers or funding bodies. The principle of self-care means that it is right also for youth workers to attend to this for themselves and for each other, to make claims for resources on their own behalf, and to actively seek proper conditions and rewards for their work. Self-harm does not just mean cutting yourself; occupational self-harm can be just as pathological.

Self-care does not, in principle, contradict the fundamental idea of the young person as the primary client. The key resource that youth workers have is themselves. It is difficult to be attentive, creative and positive in your engagement with young people when you are worried about whether you will have a roof over your head in the immediate future, or your car is constantly breaking down, or you have worked 14 days straight without a break, or haven't had a full night's sleep for a week. Not only are most people irritable and reactive under these kinds of conditions, but their fine perception and powers of observation drop away, they lose insight, they take offence where no offence is meant. In short, they become destructive in interpersonal relationships, make poor decisions and are difficult to work with. Youth work requires finely tuned interpersonal skills and lots of patience. If you are running rough, young people are unlikely to get the best from you. In fact, a typical burnout reaction is to resent young people and start to blame them for their own situation (Maslach and Jackson 1981).

Turnover also means short periods in a position. Young people don't get the chance to develop a long-term relationship with their youth worker, building trust and providing room for deeper challenges, because they were gone within a year.

They then have to educate yet another worker into the subtleties of the geography, relationships, conflicts and tensions of their local area. The organisation has to divert scarce resources into advertising, training and induction. More broadly, if there is constant turnover in our field because wages and conditions are too poor for people to be able to make a reasonable living, young people will have to constantly work with youth workers who are inexperienced, managed by others who haven't been around that much longer (Hartje et al. 2008). The constant brain-drain of experience and intelligence that comes from that turnover also keeps the field constantly juvenile and dominated by funding bureaucrats, local government authority officers and other professionals just because they have been around longer. For young people's sake, youth workers need to be paid properly, have decent working conditions and a reasonable career structure. Young people need youth workers to hang around, to be in for the long haul.

There can be tensions. It is easier for youth workers to work nine-to-five and spend evenings and weekends with their families and friends. But young people are in school for most of that time. It is important to them that youth workers are available after four. A youth service organised around the convenience of workers probably doesn't have the balance right. On the other hand, a service that has its workers out six nights a week is going to have a problem with them maintaining good relationships with family and friends, keeping healthy and sane, and arriving for work each day keen and positive and available to the young people they meet.

Strategies for self-care

1. **Take it seriously**. This might mean considering a number of things beyond the hours that you work and the salary you are paid. The pattern of the youth work day and the style of engagement with young people has often meant that youth workers drink too much coffee and smoke too many cigarettes. If you work a lot of evenings, a good diet can be hard to maintain, and a drink to relax after work easily becomes three or four. It can be hard to find time for regular exercise. If we were working with young people with that kind of lifestyle, we would want to intervene.

2. **Join the union**. Wages and conditions are often poor in youth work because funding levels are low. But funders set funding levels low because they can. With stronger unions comes a stronger and more stable set of norms for what youth workers ought to be paid. Stronger unions come from greater coverage of the sector (in other words, more members) and from active membership. So wages for youth workers are low also because youth workers don't do anything about it. If wages were better, funding would adjust to cover them. We would urge young workers to be members of a union, but youth workers' own rate of unionisation is generally woeful.

3. **Organise supervision**. As well as line management, many professions have a system of professional or clinical supervision. That means there is someone apart from your line manager, inside or outside the organisation, to whom you are accountable for your professional development and integrity,

and to whom you can go when you need to talk about issues that you don't want to talk to your line manager about. Traditions on this matter vary from country to country and from organisation to organisation. But establishing professional supervision is best practice. If your organisation doesn't have capacity to offer it internally, pay an external supervisor. If your organisation isn't interested, organise one yourself, even if you have to pay them yourself. About once a month is good.

4. **Log your time.** With a professional practice as unstructured and informal as youth work often is, it is very easy to lose time and find yourself at the end of a week or a month having no idea what you have achieved or where the time went. Make time at the end of every day to log what you spent your time on – it only takes five minutes. I have often categorised time into relevant classifications, so I can see the breakdown of my work and make decisions about the right balance. For example, *contact* (i.e. face-to-face work with young people), *networking* outside the agency, *meetings* inside the agency, *administration*, *research*. Keep a running total for the week. My supervisor has sometimes required me to log the amount of time I actually had off in the week as well, just to make sure that I have had enough.

5. **Promote a healthy workplace culture.** As a healthy workplace won't support laziness, inefficiency or corruption, it should also not support over-work or pathologies of victimhood or masochism, or the discourses that promote them. Working very hard for short periods is fine and sometimes necessary, but should not be supported by our workplace colleagues as a lifestyle. Workaholism should not be affirmed: it is no virtue.

6. **Know yourself, self-monitor.** Learn to recognise the signs for when you are working too hard: that tickle in your throat, the feeling of really not wanting to go to work, wishing you were sick so you could stay home, a certain tone in your voice, a private (or not so private) self-pity, endless talk about how hard you are working or how poorly you are paid, finding that you don't like the young people you work with and wish they would go away. If you are not good at self-regulation, contract family, partners, colleagues or friends to watch out for when you are starting to burn out. Give them the power to confront you, and agree ahead of time to listen to them when they do. Or, undertake one of the many tests of professional burnout around (e.g. Maslach and Jackson 1981). And do something about it. It can take a long long time to recover from entrenched burnout. We lose good workers all the time from our field because of it.

Conclusion

At the heart of a good youth worker is a beautiful spirit, a quality of connection that is positive, hopeful, good. It is often this that is transformative, projecting a possibility that young people can see for a way to be different. But the situations that youth workers have to deal with are often not beautiful: we often confront horrifying neglect and abuse, disturbing levels of violence, naked, hard-core damage to people that we care for and respect, the wanton waste of human life. And often enough, the experience of personal injustice or violence directed at us in the workplace or the community.

A youth worker's quality of spirit needs to be nurtured, maintained and protected. Without care, it can become scarred, cynical and bitter, and 90% of the capacity for doing anything worthwhile is lost. Then it is time to get out. The most important resource for the young people that you work with is you: intelligent, alert, wise, compassionate, engaged, skilful, insightful, well-informed, well-connected, articulate, creative, productive, confident you. Creating and maintaining this beast in the midst of high pressure and often poor resource provision needs work and constant attention. Good diet, enough sleep, exercise, enough time for reflection, good friends, supportive partners and family, wise mentors, enough money managed well, a nourishing environment, enough art and new inspiration, new learning, taking risks. We know these things. We work with young people to try to get them in place all the time. We need also to practise what we preach, not just because it is good in itself, but because it significantly affects the quality of service we give to young people, our resilience in the face of difficulty and pressure, and our recovery time when bad things happen.

All of these things take time and, typically, time is something that youth workers don't have a lot of. But young people need youth workers who are skilled, knowledgeable, healthy and fully present right now, and into the future. Of course, some of us won't be youth workers all our lives, and that is fine. Some will do a stint and leave, some will move in and out, but it is critical that some of us are still engaged with young people and the struggles they face a decade or two from now. It is a lovely experience to meet old youth workers, now in their 60s or 70s, who are as fresh and positive (and just a little wicked) as the day they first came through the door. Some of this resilience is just them: they are just irrepressible. But it is also about sufficient attention to the bottom line, about balance.

Often, youth workers have not been good at claiming the resources we need to do our job. It is a truism that professionals often assimilate the qualities of their clients, a process sometimes referred to in the literature as *parallel process* (Williams 1997). Young people are not good at organising in their own interests, although they are much better at organising to help other people. Youth workers are the same (Yohalem 2002). Youth workers will work hard to empower other people, but have not always been good at empowering themselves or their own profession. As the ancient challenge says: 'Physician, heal [or in this case, empower] thyself'.

REFERENCES

Arnett, J. (ed.) (2002). *Readings on Adolescence and Emerging Adulthood*. Upper Saddle River, NJ: Pearson Education.

Banks, S. (1999). Ethics and the youth worker, in S. Banks (ed.), *Ethical Issues in Youth Work*. London: Routledge. pp. 3–20.

Banks, S. (2003). From oaths to rulebooks: A critical examination of codes of ethics for the social professions. *European Journal of Social Work*, 6(2): 133–44.

Banks, S. (2004). *Ethics, Accountability and the Social Professions*. Basingstoke: Palgrave Macmillan.

Barwick, H. (2006). *Youth Work Today: A Review of the Issues and Challenges*. Wellington, New Zealand: Ministry of Youth Development.

Batliwala, S. (2007). Taking the power out of empowerment: An experiential account. *Development in Practice*, 17(4 & 5), August: 557–565.

Baudrillard, J. (1983). *Simulations and in the Shadow of the Silent Majorities*. New York: Semiotext(e).

Bauman, Z. (1992). *Intimations of Postmodernity*. London: Routledge.

Bayles, M. (1981). *Professional Ethics*. Belmont: Wadsworth Publishing.

BBC (2003). The Hippocratic Oath. Retrieved 20 June 2008 from: www.bbc.co.uk/dna/h2g2/A1103798.

Beck, U. (1992). *Risk Society: Towards a New Modernity*. London: Sage.

Belliotti, R. (1993). Sex, in P. Singer (ed.), *A Companion to Ethics*. London: Blackwell. pp. 315–326.

Benedict, R. (1935). *Patterns of Culture*. London: Routledge and Kegan Paul.

Bessant, J. (2004). Youth work: The Loch Ness Monster and professionalism. *Youth Studies Australia*, 23(4): 26–33.

Bessant, J., Sercombe, H. and Watts, R. (1998). *Youth Studies: An Australian Perspective*. Melbourne: Addison-Wesley Longman.

Bok, S. (1978). *Lying: Moral Choice in Public and Private Life*. Hassocks, Sussex: Harvester Press.

Bouthoutsos, J. et al. (1983). Sexual intimacy between psychotherapists and patients. *Professional Psychology: Research and Practice*, 14(2): 185–196.

Brandeis, L. D. (1914). *Business: A Profession*. Boston, MA: Small and Maynard.

Brew, J. M. (1957). *Youth and Youth Groups*. London: Faber & Faber.

British Medical Association (2008). Confidentiality and disclosure of health information tool kit. Retrieved 24 January 2009 from: www.bma.org.uk/health_promotion_ethics/confidentiality/ConfToolKit08.jsp.

Bronfenbrenner, U. (1979). *The Ecology of Human Development: Experiments by Nature and Design*. Cambridge, MA: Harvard University Press.

Buber, M. (1965). Guilt and guilt feelings, in M. Buber, *The Knowledge of Man*. New York: Harper and Row. pp. 121–148.

Bunch, C. (1987). *Passionate Politics: Feminist Theory in Action*. Basingstoke: Macmillan/St Martin's Press.

Campbell, T. (1988). *Justice*. Basingstoke: Macmillan.

Carmody, M. (2009a). *Sex and Ethics: Young People and Ethical Sex*. Melbourne: Macmillan.

Carmody, M. (2009b). *Sex and Ethics: The Sexual Ethics Education Program for Young People*. Melbourne: Macmillan.

Carmody, M. and Willis, K. (2006). Developing ethical sexual lives: Young people, sex and sexual assault prevention. Sydney: University of Western Sydney.

Chapman, M. and Chinn, N. (1982). *Mickey*. Performed by Toni Basil. Santa Monica, CA: A&M Records.

Chief Secretary to the Treasury (2003). *Every Child Matters*. Norwich: HMSO.

Commonwealth Youth Programme (2005). *Commonwealth Youth Programme Strategic Plan 2006–2008*. London: Commonwealth Youth Programme.

Conde, C. (2004). The Foresight Saga: Risk, litigiousness and negligence law reforms. *Policy*, 20(3): 28–34.

Corey, G., Corey, M. and Callanan, P. (2007). *Issues and Ethics in the Helping Professions*. Belmont, CA: Thomson.

Crimmens, D. and Whalen, A. (1999). Rights-based approaches to working with young people, in S. Banks (ed.), *Ethical Issues in Youth Work*. London: Routledge. pp. 164–180.

Cuff, E., et al. (1998). *Perspectives in Sociology*. London: Routledge.

Daniel, S. (1997). *Confidentiality and Young People*. Leicester: Centre for Social Action/ De Montfort University.

Davies, B. (1999). *A History of the Youth Service in England (Vol. 1)*. Leicester: National Youth Agency.

Davies, B. (2005). Youth work: A manifesto for our times. *Youth & Policy*, 88 (Summer): 5–28.

Davies, B. and Merton, B. (2009). Squaring the circle? Findings of a 'modest inquiry' into the state of youth work practice in a changing policy environment. Leicester: DeMontfort University.

Davis, C. (1988). Philosophical foundations of interdisciplinarity in caring for the elderly, or the willingness to change your mind. *Physiotherapy Practice*, 4: 23–25.

Dawson, A. (1994). Professional codes of practice and ethical conduct. *Journal of Applied Philosophy*, 11(2): 125–133.

deLeon, P. and Green, M. T. (2002). New Public Management and political corruption: Establishing the parameters. *The 2002 International Public Management Network Conference*. Universita degli Studi di Siena.

Dominelli, L. (2007). The postmodern 'turn' in social work: The challenges of identity and equality. *The International Online-Only Journal*, 5.

Donner, M. B., Vande Creek, L., Gonsiorek, J. C. and Fisher, C. B. (2008). Balancing confidentiality: Protecting privacy and protecting the public. *Professional Psychology: Research and Practice*, 39(3): 369–376.

Draft Committee for the International Leadership Coalition for Professional Child and Youth Care (1995). Ethics of Child and Youth Care Professionals: A code developed by the Draft Committee for the International Leadership Coalition for Professional Child and Youth Care. *Child & Youth Care Forum*, 24(6): 371–378.

Durkheim, E. (1957). *Professional Ethics and Public Morals*. London: Routledge and Kegan Paul.

Dyhouse, C. (1981). *Girls Growing Up in Late Victorian and Edwardian England*. London: Routledge and Kegan Paul.

Ebenstein, A. (2001). *Friedrich Hayek: A Biography*. Basingstoke: Palgrave Macmillan.

Epstein, R. (2007). *The Case against Adolescence: Rediscovering the Adult in Every Teen*. Sanger, CA: Quill Driver Books.

Foucault, M. (1984). *The History of Sexuality: An Introduction*. Harmondsworth: Penguin.

Freeman, K. (ed.) (1948). *Ancilla to the Pre-Socratic Philosophers*. Oxford: Basil Blackwell.

Frost, N., Robinson, M. and Anning, A. (2005). Social workers in multidisciplinary teams: Issues and dilemmas for professional practice. *Child & Family Social Work*, 10(3): 187–196.

Garofalo, C., Geuras, D., Lynch, T. D. and Lynch, C. E. (2001). Applying virtue ethics to the challenge of corruption. *The Innovation Journal*, 6(2), www.innovation.cc/peer-reviewed/virture-ethics-corruption.htm

Gilligan, C. (1977) In a different voice: Women's conception of the self and of morality, *Harvard Educational Review*, 47(4): 481–517.

Gillis, J. (1974). *Youth and History: Tradition and Change in European Age Relations, 1770–present*. New York: Academic Press.

Gillon, R. (1985). 'Primum non nocere' and the principle of non-maleficence. *British Medical Journal*, 291: 130–131.

Gottlieb, M. C. (1993). Avoiding exploitive dual relationships: A decision-making model. *Psychotherapy*, 30(1): 41–48.

Greenwood, E. (1957). Attributes of a profession. *Social Work*, 3(2): 44–55.

Griffiths, M. (2000). Collaboration and partnership in question: Knowledge, politics and practice. *Journal of Education Policy*, 15(4): 383–395.

Guardian (2003). German internet cannibal begins murder trial. *The Guardian*. Retrieved 3 June 2008 from: www.guardian.co.uk/world/2003/dec/03/germany.

Gunson, D. and Collins, C. (1997). From the I to the we: Discourse ethics, identity, and the pragmatics of partnership in the West of Scotland. *Communication Theory*, 7(4): 278–300.

Habermas, J. (1994). *Justification and Application: Remarks on Discourse Ethics*. Cambridge, MA: MIT Press.

Haebich, A. (1992). *For Their Own Good: Aborigines and Government in the South West of Western Australia 1900–40*. Perth: University of Western Australia Press.

Hall, K. (2001). Sexualization of the doctor–patient relationship: Is it ever ethically permissible? *Family Practice*, 18(5): 511–515.

Harrison, R. and Wise, C. (eds) (2005). *Working with Young People*. London: Sage/The Open University.

Hartje, J. A. et al. (2008). Youth worker characteristics and self-reported competency as predictors of intent to continue working with youth. *Child Youth Care Forum*, 37: 27–41.

Havighurst, R. J. and Dreyer, P. H. (1975). *Youth*. Chicago: University of Chicago Press.

Hay, L. (1987). *You Can Heal Your Life*. Concord, MA: Specialist Publications.

Hayek, F. (1978). *The Constitution of Liberty*. Chicago: University of Chicago Press.

Hewison, A. and Sim, J. (1998). Managing interprofessional working: Using codes of ethics as a foundation. *Journal of Interprofessional Care*, 12(3): 309–321.

Hobbes, T. (1996, orig. 1651). *Leviathan*. Oxford: Oxford University Press.

Hume, D. (1739/1985) *A Treatise of Human Nature: Being an Attempt to Introduce the Experimental Method of Reasoning into Moral Subjects*. London: Penguin.

Huxham, C. and Vangen, S. (2000). Ambiguity, complexity and dynamics in the management of collaboration. *Human Relations*, 53(6): 771–806.

Illich, I. et al. (1977). *Disabling Professions*. New York: Marion Boyars.

Imam, U. (1999). Youth workers and mediators and interpreters: Ethical issues in work with black young people, in S. Banks (ed.), *Ethical Issues in Youth Work*. London: Routledge. pp. 125–144.

Institut für Sozialarbeit und Sozialpädagogik (2007). *The Socioeconomic Scope of Youth Work in Europe*. Strasbourg: Youth Partnership of the European Commission & the Council of Europe.

Irvine, R., Kerridge, I., McPhee, J. and Freeman, S. (2002). Interprofessionalism and ethics: Consensus or clash of cultures? *Journal of Interprofessional Care*, 16(3): 199–210.

Jeffs, T. (2005). Citizenship, youth work and democratic renewal. *The Encyclopedia of Informal Education*. Retrieved 17 February 2009 from: www.infed.org/association/citizenship_youth_work_democratic_renewal.

Jeffs, T. and Smith, M. (1999a). Resourcing youth work: Dirty hands and tainted money, in S. Banks (ed.), *Ethical Issues in Youth Work*. London: Routledge. pp. xxx–xxx.

Jeffs, T. and Smith, M. (1999b). The problem of youth for youth work. *Youth and Policy*, 62: 45–66.

Jeffs, T. and Smith, M. (2005). *Informal Education: Conversation, Democracy and Learning*. Nottingham: Educational Heretics Press.

Johnston, J. (1974). *Lesbian Nation*. New York: Simon & Schuster.

Kamiya, G. (1997). Cablinasian like me. Retrieved 20 March 2009 from: www.salon.com/april97/tiger970430.html.

Kant, I. (1781/2007) *Critique of Pure Reason*. London: Penguin Classics.

Kant, I. (1788/2005). *The Critique of Practical Reason*. Sioux Falls, South Dakota: Nu Vision Publications.

Keay, D. (1987, Sept 23) Aids, Education and the year 2000!, *Woman's Own*, 8–10.

Kett, J. (1977). *Rites of Passage: Adolescence in America 1790 to the present*. New York: Basic Books.

Koehn, D. (1994). *The Ground of Professional Ethics*. London: Routledge.

Koehn, D. (1998). *Rethinking Feminist Ethics*. London: Routledge.

Lenin, V. I. (1919/1972). The state: A lecture delivered at the Sverdlov University. *Lenin's Collected Works* (Vol. 29). Moscow: Progress Publishers. pp. 470–488.

Lewin, K. (1951). *Field Theory in Social Science: Selected Theoretical Papers*. Edited by D. Cartwright. New York: Harper & Row.

Lichtenberg, J. (1996). What are codes of ethics for?, in M. Coady and S. Bloch (eds), *Codes of Ethics and the Professions*. Melbourne: Melbourne University Press. pp. 13–27.

Martin, L. (2002). *The Invisible Table: Perspectives on Youth and Youthwork in New Zealand*. Wellington: Dunmore Press.

Martin, L. (2006). *Real Work: A Report from the National Research Project on the State of Youth Work in Aotearoa*. Christchurch, New Zealand: National Youth Workers' Network of New Zealand.

Martin, M. (1989). *Everyday Morality: An Introduction to Applied Ethics*. Belmont, CA: Wadsworth.

Marx, K. (1935). *The Eighteenth Brumaire of Napoleon Bonaparte*. London: Martin Lawrence Ltd.

Maslach, C. and Jackson, S. (1981). The measurement of experienced burnout. *Journal of Occupational Behaviour*, 2: 99–113.

Mattingly, M. A. (1995). Ethics of Child and Youth Care Professionals: A code developed by the Draft Committee for the International Leadership Coalition for Professional Child and Youth Care. *Child and Youth Care Forum*, 24(6): 371–378.

Mattingly, M. A. (2005). Developing professional ethics for child and youth care work: Assuming responsibility for the quality of care. *Child & Youth Care Forum*, 24(6): 379–391.

May, W. (1975). Code and covenant or philanthropy and contract. *Hastings Center Report*, 5(6): 29–38.

Melton, G. (1983). Toward 'personhood' for adolescents. *American Psychologist*, January: 99–101.

Merton, B. et al. (2004). *An Evaluation of the Impact of Youth Work in England*. Nottingham: De Montfort University Youth Affairs Unit/Department for Education and Skills.

Midgley, M. (1993a). *Can't We Make Moral Judgements?* New York: St Martin's Press.

Midgley, M. (1993b). Trying out one's new sword, in C. Sommers and F. Sommers (eds), *Vice and Virtue in Everyday life*. Forth Worth, TX: Harcourt Brace College Publishers. pp. 174–180.

Ministry for Youth Development (2001). *Supporting the Positive Development of Young People – A Discussion Document for Consultation on a Youth Development Strategy Aotearoa: Summary Analysis of Responses from Agencies and Adults on the Consultation Document*. Wellington, New Zealand: Ministry for Youth Development.

Ministry of Education (1960). *The Youth Service in England and Wales*. The Albemarle Report. London: HMSO.

Morgan, S. and Banks, S. (1999). The youth worker as confidante: Issues of welfare and trust, in S. Banks (ed.), *Ethical Issues in Youth Work*. London: Routledge. pp. 145–163.

Muuss, R. (1996). *Theories of Adolescence*. New York: McGraw-Hill.

National Youth Agency (2002). *Ethical Conduct in Youth Work: A Statement of Values and Principles from The National Youth Agency*. Leicester: The National Youth Agency.

National Youth Agency (nd). Staying Safe. Retrieved 10 February 2009 from: www.nya.org.uk/information/100594/100629/108816/gpstayingsafe/.

National Youth Workers Conference (1977). Jasper Declaration. *National Youth Workers Conference*. Adelaide.

National Youth Workers Network Aotearoa (2008). *Code of Ethics for Youth Work in Aotearoa New Zealand*. First edition. Retrieved 1 July 2008 from: www.youthworkers.net.nz/CoE0book.pdf.

Noddings, N. (2002). *Educating Moral People: A Caring Alternative to Character Education*. Williston, VT: Teachers College Press.

Nozick, R. (1974). *Anarchy, State, and Utopia*. Oxford: Blackwell.

Papps, E. and Ramsden, I. (1996). Cultural safety in nursing: The New Zealand Experience. *International Journal for Quality in Health Care*, 8: 491–497.

Patterson, J. (1992). A Maori concept of collective responsibility, in G. Oddie and R. W. Perrett. (eds), *Justice, Ethics and New Zealand Society*. Auckland: Oxford University Press.

Pittman, K. and Fleming, W. E. (1991). *A New Vision: Promoting Youth Development*. Washington, DC: Center for Youth Development and Policy Research.

Poynting, S. and White, R. (2004) 'Youthwork: Challenging the soft cop syndrome. *Youth Studies Australia*, 23(4): 39–46.

Punzo, V. C. (1969). *Reflective Naturalism*. New York: Macmillan.

Quixley, S. and Doostkhah, S. (2007). *Conservatising Youth Work? Dangers of Adopting a Code of Ethics*. Brisbane: Youth Affairs Network of Queensland.

Raiment, B. (1994). *Confidential: Developing Confidential Policies in Youth Counselling and Advisory Services*. London: Youth Access/Wandsworth Youth Advisory Service.

Rand, A. (1997). *Journals of Ayn Rand*. New York: Dutton/Penguin.

Rand, A. and Branden, N. (1964). *The Virtue of Selfishness: A New Concept of Egoism*. New York: Signet/New American Library.

Ranelagh, J. (1991). *Thatcher's People: An Insider's Account of the Politics, the Power, and the Personalities*. London: Harper Collins.

Reiman, J. H. (1990). *Justice and Modern Moral Philosophy*. New Haven, CT: Yale University Press.

Rhodes, M. (1986). *Ethical Dilemmas in Social Work Practice*. Boston, MA: Routledge and Kegan Paul.

Roberts, J. (2009). *Youth Work Ethics*. Exeter: Learning Matters.

Rogers, C. R. (1961). *On Becoming a Person. A Therapist's View of Psychotherapy*. Boston: Houghton Mifflin.

Rose-Ackerman, S. (1999). *Corruption and Government: Causes, Consequences and Reform*. Cambridge: Cambridge University Press.

Rousseau, J. J. (1762/2006). *Political Writings: Containing the Social Contract, Considerations on the Government of Poland, Constitutional Project for Corsica, Part I*. Madison, WI: University of Wisconsin Press.

Royal College of Nursing (2005). Confidentiality: RCN guidance for occupational health nurses. Retrieved 24 January 2009 from: www.rcn.org.uk/__data/assets/pdf_file/0003/78582/002043.pdf.

Sallah, M. and Howson, C. (eds) (2007). *Working with Black Young People*. Lyme Regis: Russell House Publishing.

Sapin, K. (2009). *Essential Skills for Youth Work Practice*. London: Sage.

Schank, J. A. and Skovholt, T. M. (1997). Dual-relationship dilemmas of rural and small-community psychologists. *Professional Psychology: Research and Practice*, 28 (I): 44–49.

Schlegel, A. (2009). Cross-cultural issues in the study of adolescent development, in L. Steinberg and R. Lerner (eds), *Handbook of Adolescent Psychology: Contextual Influences on Adolescent Development* (vol. 2). New York: Wiley-Blackwell.

Schnapp, A. (1997). Images of young people in the Greek city-state, in G. Levi and J.-C. Schmitt (eds), *A History of Young People in the West: Ancient and Medieval Rites of Passage*. Cambridge, MA: The Belknapp Press of Harvard University Press.

Scottish Executive (2004). *Working and Learning Together to Build Stronger Communities*. Edinburgh: Communities Scotland.

Scruton, R. (2001). *Sexual Desire*. London: Phoenix Press.

Scruton, R. (2003). The moral birds and the bees: sex and marriage, properly understood. *National Review*, 55(17) 37–39.

Searle-Chaterjee, M. (ed.) (2000). *Community: Description, Debate and Dilemma*. Birmingham: Venture Press.

Secretary of State for Education and Skills (2005). *Youth Matters*. Norwich: HMSO.

Seig, A. (1976). Why adolescence occurs, in H. Thornburg (ed.), *Contemporary Adolescence: Readings*. Monterey, CA: Brooks/Cole.

Sercombe, H. (1989). *Youth: Towards a Sociological Definition*. Perth: Youth Work Studies, Western Australian College of Advanced Education.

Sercombe, H. (1996). Naming youth: The construction of the youth category. DPhil dissertation. *Philosophy, Politics and Sociology*. Murdoch University, Perth.

Sercombe, H. (1997a). The youth work contract: Professionalism and ethics. *Youth Studies Australia*, 16(4): 17–21.

Sercombe, H. (1997b). The contradictory position of youth workers in the public sphere. *Youth Studies Australia*, 16(1): 43–47.

Sercombe, H. (1997c). Clearing the streets: Youth curfews and social order. *Just Policy*, 10 (June): 14–19.

Sercombe, H. (2004). *Millen Street Policy Manual: A Model Policy Manual for a Youth Work Service*. Kalgoorlie: Centrecare Goldfields.

Sercombe, H. (2006). Going bush: Youth work in rural settings. *Youth Studies Australia*, 25(3): 9–16.

Sercombe, H. (2008). Living in two camps: The strategies Goldfields Aboriginal people use to manage in the Aboriginal economy and the mainstream economy at the same time. *Australian Aboriginal Studies*, December: 16–31.

Sercombe, H. (2009a). The 'teen brain' research: Critical perspectives. *Youth and Policy*, 101 (Summer).

Sercombe, H. (2009b). The gift and the trap: Working the 'teen brain' into our concept of youth. *Journal of Adolescent Research* (in press).

Sercombe, H. (2010). Youth workers as professionals: managing dual relationships and maintaining boundaries, in S. Banks (ed.), *Ethical Issues in Youth Work*. London: Routledge.

Sercombe, H., Omaji, P., Drew, N., Love, T. and Cooper, T. (2002). Youth and the future: Effective youth services for the year 2015. *National Youth Affairs Research Scheme*. Hobart: National Clearinghouse for Youth Studies.

Sercombe, H. and Paus, T. (2009). The 'teen brain' research: Implications for practitioners. *Youth and Policy*, 103(Summer): 25–38.

Sinclair, A. (1996). Codes in the workplace: Organisational versus professional codes, in M. Coady and S. Bloch (eds), *Codes of Ethics and the Professions*. Melbourne: Melbourne University Press. pp. 88–108.

Smart, J. J. C. (1973). An outline of a system of utilitarian ethics, in J. J. C. Smart and B. Williams (eds), *Utilitarianism: For and Against*. Cambridge: Cambridge University Press. pp. 3–76.

Smith, M. K. (1999/2002). Youth work: An introduction. *The Encyclopedia of Informal Education*. Retrieved 31 March 2008 from: www.infed.org/youthwork/b-yw.htm.

Smith, M. K. (2002). Transforming youth work – Resourcing Excellent Youth Services: A Critique. *The Informal Education Homepage*. Retrieved 19 August 2008 from: www.infed.org/youthwork/transforming_youth_work_2.htm.

Smith, M. K. and Doyle, M. E. (2002). The Albemarle Report and the development of youth work in England and Wales. *The Encyclopedia of Informal Education*. Retrieved 31 March 2008 from: www.infed.org/youthwork/albemarle_report.htm.

Sommers, C. (1985). Teaching the virtues, in C. Sommers and F. Sommers (eds), *Vice and Virtue in Everyday Life: Introductory Readings in Ethics*. Fort Worth, TX: Harcourt Brace College Publishers. pp. 677–687.

Sommers, C. and Sommers, F. (eds) (1985). *Vice and Virtue in Everyday Life*. Fort Worth, TX: Harcourt Brace College Publishers.

Spence, J. and Devanney, C. (2006). *Youth Work: Voices of Practice*. Leicester: The National Youth Agency.

Springhall, J. (1984). The origins of adolescence. *Youth and Policy*, 2(3): 20–35.

Springhall, J. (1986). *Coming of Age: Adolescence in Britain, 1860–1960*. Dublin: Gill and Macmillan.

Standards Council for Community Learning and Development (2009). *Competence in Community Learning and Development: Draft Refreshed Competences*. Glasgow: Standards Council for Community Learning and Development.

Thompson, E. P. (1971). The moral economy of the English crowd in the 18th century. *Past & Present*, 50: 76–136.

Thomson, C. (2006). Caught up in the curfew: The Hamilton Child Safety Initiative remembered. Retrieved 20 March 2009 from: www.cjscotland.org.uk/index.php/cjscotland/dynamic_page/?title=hamilton_curfew.

Tomsett, C. and Groves, M. (2006). *The Cambridgeshire Youth Work Curriculum*. Cambridge: Cambridgeshire County Council.

Transport and General Workers' Union (2008). Professional Development for Youth Workers. Retrieved 27 June 2008 from: www.tgwu.org.uk/Templates/News.asp?NodeID =94383&int1stParentNodeID=42438&int2ndParentNodeID=42438&Action=Display.

Tucker, S. (2004). Youth working: Professional identities given, received or contested?, in J. Roche, S. Tucker, R. Thomson and R. Flynn (eds), *Youth in Society*. London: Sage/Open University. pp. 81–90.

VanRee, F. (1999). Intimate relationships between young people and adults: Are there criteria for a positive experience? *Koinos Magazine*, 24(4): Accessed 26 August 2009 from http://www.p-100g.info/English/v_ree_criteria.html.

Villarruel, F., Perkins, D., Borden, L. and Keith, J. (eds) (2002). *Community Youth Development: Programs, Policies and Practices*. Thousand Oaks, CA: Sage.

Vygotsky, L. S. (1962). *Thought and Language*. Cambridge, MA: MIT Press.

Vygotsky, L. S. (1978). *Mind and Society: The Development of Higher Psychological Processes*. Cambridge, MA: Harvard University Press.

Walker, J. A. (2002). The essential youth worker: Supports and opportunities for professional success, in F. Villarruel, D. Perkins, L. Borden and J. Keith (eds), *Community Youth Development: Programs, Policies and Practices*. Thousand Oaks, CA: Sage. pp. 373–93.

Weindling, P. J. (2005). *Nazi Medicine and the Nuremberg Trials: From Medical War Crimes to Informed Consent*. London: Palgrave Macmillan.

White, R. (1987). Subversives ...or soft cops? Notes toward an examination of the politics of youth work. Paper presented at the Conference of the Nationwide Workers with Youth Forum, Adelaide.

White, R. (1990). *No Space of Their Own*. Cambridge: Cambridge University Press.

Williams, A. B. (1997). On parallel process in social work supervision. *Clinical Social Work Journal*, 25(4): 425–435.

Wyn, J. and White, R. (1997). *Rethinking Youth*. St Leonards: Allen and Unwin.

Yohalem, N. (2002). Adults who make a difference: Identifying the skills and characteristics of successful youth workers, in F. Villarruel, D. Perkins, L. Borden and J. Keith (eds), *Community Youth Development: Programs, Policies and Practices*. Thousand Oaks, CA: Sage. pp. 358–72.

Young, K. (1999). The youth worker as guide, philosopher and friend: The realities of participation and empowerment, in S. Banks (ed.), *Ethical Issues in Youth Work*. London: Routledge. pp. 77–92.

Young, K. (2006). *The Art of Youth Work*. Lyme Regis: Russell House Publishing.

Younggren, J. N. (2003). Ethical decision–making and dual relationships. Retrieved 14 January 2009 from: www. kspope.com/dual/younggren.php#copy.

Youth Affairs Council of Australia (1983). *Creating Tomorrow Today: A Youth Policy Report based on Nationwide Consultation*. St Kilda South, Victoria: Youth Affairs Council of Australia.

Youth Affairs Council of Victoria (2008). *Code of Ethical Practice – A First Step for the Victorian Youth Sector*. Melbourne: Youth Affairs Council of Victoria.

Youth Affairs Council of Western Australia (2003). *A Code of Ethics for Youth Work*. Retrieved 1 July 2008 from: www.yacwa.org.au/files/Code%20of%20Ethics%20 Booklet.pdf.

Youthlink Scotland (2005). Statement on the Nature and Purpose of Youth Work. Retrieved 22 March 2008 from: www.youthlink.co.uk/docs/Youth%20Work%20 Statement%20leaflet.pdf.

Zukav, G. (1990). *The Seat of the Soul*. New York: Simon & Schuster.

INDEX